Christianity with

CHRISTIANITY WITHOUT ABSOLUTES

Reinhold Bernhardt

SCM PRESS LTD

Translated by John Bowden from the German *Zwischen Grössenwahn, Fanatismus und Bekennermut. Für ein Christentum ohne Absolutheitsanspruch*, published 1994 by Kreuz Verlag, Stuttgart.

0 334 02566 4

First British edition published 1994
by SCM Press Ltd,
26-30 Tottenham Road, London N1 4BZ

Typeset at The Spartan Press Ltd, Lymington, Hants
and printed in Great Britain by
Biddles Ltd, Guildford and King's Lynn

Contents

'No sin is so reprehensible as to despise one's brother because his creed is a different one'

(Bayezid Bastâmi, a Persian Sufi master of the ninth century)

Preface

Theology in the Service of Religious Peace

We live in a time in which two tendencies are converging and producing a dangerous situation. On the one hand, at present the fronts between the religions are hardening in a dramatic way. Concern for one's own religion is prevailing over openness to others; provincialism is winning out over globalism. We can find increased fundamentalist tendencies in all religions and world-views – including late-twentieth century Christian Protestantism. On the other hand, the adherents of the religions are increasingly members of multi-religious societies. There are still relatively homogeneous religious landscapes at best in the Muslim world. By contrast, non-Christian religious communities have long been established in the Western world. In Europe the largest among them is that of Islam, with approximately twenty million adherents. We must assume that this tendency towards religious pluralism will intensify in the future.

Pluralism in culture and religion by no means automatically produces a climate of tolerance and openness between the faith communities. On the contrary, there can be sharp dividing lines, particularly where religious groups or confessions live together in a small space.

Thus multi-religious societies are always fragile and endangered structures. All too quickly, social conflicts combine with religious confessions and break out in a brutal way. There are many terrifying examples of the collapse of multi-religious societies which once functioned: for example the conflict in and around Bosnia, where Catholic Christians, Orthodox Christians and Muslims are fighting one another and separating from one another, or the reconquest of

Moorish Spain by the Christians 500 years ago as a result of which Jews and Muslims were driven out. Consequently a flourishing culture became a wilderness. Nor should it be forgotten that for centuries Germany, too, was a multi-religious society in which a large non-Christian group, the Jews, lived until they were driven out and exterminated. The hatred against this people was always also hatred against their religion – and from the beginning it was fomented by the teachers of Christian religion.

At all times Christians have seen their task as that of demonstrating the uniqueness and superiority of the Christian religion to other religions. Here they have often laid the spiritual foundation for hostility, especially towards Jews and Muslims. In the history of Christianity the theological *condemnation* of a religion has always been closely connected with the *behaviour* of Christians towards members of that religion. Where a religion was condemned theologically as an monster of Satan, like Islam in the Middle Ages, people also attacked its adherents in crusades. And where Christian theologians thought that the Jews were God's murderers because they had nailed Jesus to the cross, it was not long before the hatred exploded in pogroms. The violent acts between the religions were always accompanied by spiritual wars. Indeed, the more negative the verdict on the other religion, the more hostile was the behaviour towards its adherents. The relationship between the three 'brother religions' of Judaism, Christianity and Islam is the most terrifying example of this.

Multi-religious societies do not thrive as a matter of course: they need encouragement towards peaceful co-existence and mutual openness from their cultures. The co-existence of different religious communities in 'reconciled difference' must be practised with a constantly renewed concern for reciprocal dialogue. Here dialogue is more than just a conversation; it is a way of shaping a relationship, a form of coexistence.

If the religions are to live together in reconciled difference, then the individual religious communities must help to create the spiritual basis for this coexistence out of the substance of their faith (and not for tactical considerations).[1] Just as 'the peace of the world must be secured politically',[2] so peace between the religions must be secured theologically.

We live in a time in which the old enmity between Christians and

Muslims is flaring up throughout the world and is resulting in acts of violence. In this situation, Christian theology has to perform a most timely and important service for peace: it has to contribute towards the reconciliation of the religions. Not through moral appeals, but by self-critically working out the spiritual roots of violence, by demonstrating and giving theological backing to new ways of dealing with other religions drawn from the sources of its own tradition. This certainly cannot be said to be an easy task, but there is no alternative.

The demolition of dividing walls, and above all the demolition of the theological foundations of such dividing walls, is necessary if encounters in dialogue are not to be blocked from the start. And that means, first, the demolition of claims to absoluteness. But in order to be able to demolish these claims, we must learn to understand them. That is where this book seeks to make a contribution.

It seeks to make this contribution constructively, not destructively. It is not meant to be an intransigent reckoning with the 'criminal history' of Christian faith, Christian religion and the Christian church, but an apologetic attempt to distinguish the kingdom of God from the ambitions of some Christians, in history and the present, to exercise domination. I want to show up those strictly orthodox zealots who tie Jesus' message of the immediacy and nearness of God to the chariot wheels of their obsession with power and their megalomania, and thus do spiritual or even physical violence to those of other faiths. I want to oppose exaggerated *claims* to the truth, for the sake of the truth of this message.

I am grateful to Claudia Geese, Markus Merz and Andreas Weisbrod for their corrections to the draft text, for critical questions and important stimulation. Discussing their sometimes very basic objections has constantly led to exciting conversations.

I would also like to thank Raul Niemann, my editor, who prompted this book and got it going. Time and again he has been able to translate his fine sense of current problems in society, church and theology into requests which could hardly be avoided. And when – as here – a book emerged from such compelling commitment to the basic questions, he made considerable personal sacrifices for it. So this book is dedicated to him.

Introduction

Is There a 'Malignant Principle' in Christian Faith?

'The church was perfectly justified in adjudging damnation to heretics and unbelievers, for this condemnation is involved in the nature of faith . . . The believer has God *for him*, the unbeliever, *against him* . . . But that which has God against it is worthless, rejected, reprobate . . . Hence faith has fellowship with believers only; unbelievers it rejects. It is well disposed towards believers, but ill-disposed towards unbelievers. In faith there lies a malignant principle.'[1]

Is there in Christian faith itself a hostile principle which does not prompt reconciliation but fighting with other religions? If Ludwig Feuerbach is right in his claim, then any further effort to go along the way that has been indicated would be senseless from the start. If as a result of its sources Christian faith were *incapable* of peaceful relationships with other religions, then the appeal to theology to make its contribution to peace between the religions would be a hollow one. So before we take even the first step towards a Christianity with no claim to absoluteness we must deal with this objection.

There is no disputing the fact that a long trail of blood runs through the history of the Christian church(es). It extends to the present. Not only Jews and 'pagans' were victims of violent persecutions, but also Christians who had turned away from the church to form their own confessional communities.

The spiritual weapon[2] of all authority against those who believe otherwise was and always is a claim to absoluteness which regards its own religious view and practice as the only true one, i.e. as willed by God; alongside this there can be no other truth for human salvation: *no other gospel, no other name, by which we shall be saved.*

I

Here those of other faiths are judged and treated more or less compassionately, depending on where the reason for their unbelief is seen to lie: in innocent ignorance, in a culpable fall from the truth, or even in a stubbornness imposed by God. In the most favourable case it is held to their credit that they have remained in ignorance of the truth through no fault of their own, because hitherto the message of Jesus Christ has not been proclaimed to them, so that they could not know it at all: this defect was then to be made good by missionary zeal. However, if they already knew it, but did not acknowledge it and did not turn from their dangerous error, they had to be regarded as maliciously stubborn. In that case the only thing left was either to abandon them in resignation to their lostness (though Christian love of neighbour prohibited this) or to free them from their blindness by whatever means were possible. This was necessary not only for their own sakes, in order to snatch them from eternal damnation, but also and above all in order to prevent harm to the people as a whole, which could be infected by such madness.

The brutality with which the persecutors acted here can be explained not least from their view that those of other faiths were infected by demons; their false belief had to be exterminated like a plague before it could spread further. The fight was not against people of another faith but against enemies of Christ, monsters of the Antichrist and thus non-persons. Their status as human beings, i.e. as in the image of God, was in question. They were to be treated as infectious. That led to a form of cruelty which differed from the conduct of soldiers in battle. Whereas the political war was less a matter of killing individuals than of defeating the opposing army (so that it was also enough to take the enemy prisoner), in the war of faith the motive of exorcism was always in the background: the Satanic ulcer in individual human beings had to be cauterized. Fire seemed to be the best means of this.

We can see from the Requerimiento how closely missionary aid and extermination – the two attitudes towards those of another faith described above – could converge. This 'invitation' which from 1514 on the Spanish conquerors had to present to the original inhabitants of America, that had been discovered in 1492, had been composed by the Spanish crown lawyer Palacios Rubios after the Burgos consultation of 1512. This consultation had been occasioned by protests from America drawing attention to the atrocities perpetrated on the indigenous population. The document served not least to justify the conquest 'at home', in Europe. With it the claim could be maintained that not only civilization but also Christianity was being brought to the native population.[3]

With two clergy present as witnesses, a notary was to read out the following text:

'Therefore we pray and beseech you to the best of your ability to listen to what we say and take counsel for an appropriate period, to recognize the Church as the supreme Lord of the whole world and in its name the high priest, called Pope, and in his place His Majesty as Lord and King of these islands and this continent . . . and declare your agreement that the brothers in orders here present shall explain and proclaim to you what is said. If you act accordingly, then you are doing right and fulfilling your duty; then His Majesty and I will in his name treat you with love and generosity, leave you, your wives and children free and without obligation to service, so that you have control over them and yourselves as is your pleasure and as you think fit. In this instance no one will be able to compel you to become Christians, unless, having been instructed in the truth, you yourself have the wish to confess our holy Catholic faith, as almost all the inhabitants of the other islands have done. In addition His Majesty will also give you many privileges and favours and show you many graces. But if you do not do this and maliciously hesitate, then we assure you that with God's help I will take violent action against you, bring down war upon you everywhere and in every possible way, bend you under the yoke and force you to be obedient to the Church and His Majesty, make your women and children slaves, sell them, and have power over them in accordance with the command of His Majesty. We will take your property from you, harm you and do ill to you as only we can, and we shall treat you as vassals who are not obedient and submissive to their king, but obstinate and rebellious. We solemnly affirm that the bloodshed and injury which stem from this shall be your fault alone, and not that of His Majesty, myself, or these knights who have come with me.'[4]

The Indios could decide: they could either submit voluntarily, or they would be subjected by force.

Can we take this instance as proof of Feuerbach's assertion quoted at the beginning, that there is a malignant, a militant dualistic principle in Christian faith itself, which results in such treatment of those of other faiths? Was the cruel bloodshed then not a terrible *aberration* from the way through history which begins with Jesus Christ, but a work grounded in faith in Christ itself, indeed perhaps even required by this faith? Had a war of conquest waged out of a desire for gold and power sought to justify itself here with the halo of Christian mission? Or was the radical zeal of faith the driving force, which showed its true face here? After all, Jesus himself had said: 'Go into all the world and preach the gospel to the whole creation. He who believes and is baptized will be saved; but he who does not believe will be condemned' (Mark 16.15f.). Is it not necessary to conclude from this in word and deed that forcible baptism is better for non-Christians than a tolerance which makes them fall victim to God's judgment? Is this not really the foundation of an 'imperialism of salvation' which is under the delusion that it is justified in the use of force?

On the other hand the attitude of the Conquistadores is diametrically opposed to the overall picture that the Gospels hand down of Jesus' preaching. In the parables of the prodigal son, the lost sheep and the lost coin, Jesus shows us a God who seeks out the lost in boundless love. Nothing is further from this love than a forced recovery or condemnation of the lost. This boundless love, particularly for those who are thought to be lost, is directly reflected in Jesus' dealings with his fellow human beings: he transgresses all the social conventions in order to bring the lost into fellowship with God. There is no trace of force, no trace of an 'imperialism of salvation': on the contrary, in Matt.5.9 we read 'Blessed are the peacemakers, for they shall be called sons of God', and two verses later, 'Blessed are you when men revile you and persecute you.' Not, 'Blessed are the persecutors who spread the gospel among the nations with fire and sword.'

Feuerbach's diagnosis finds no support either in Jesus' belief in God or in the early Christians' belief in Christ. While Jesus and the first Christians certainly expected God's judgment, which not all men and women would withstand, they were certain that the last judgment on who would be saved and who lost lay in God's hands. And they also knew that it was not a matter of indifference to this God which judgment he made. God wills 'that *all* should be saved' (I Tim.2.4) and is concerned for each individual. That was the source of *their* mission: they were not sent to pronounce judgments of condemnation or even to carry them out, but to take part in God's sacrificial search for the lost. They preferred to accept persecution

4

and death rather than to become persecutors themselves. But it took less than three hundred years for the persecuted to become persecutors. And subsequent history offers a wealth of material to show how violence was used with a 'Christian' motive and sanctioned against those of other beliefs.

The malignant principle of which Feuerbach speaks does not lie in Jesus' belief in God or in belief in Christ. It lies in the religious self-glorification and self-righteousness which appropriates God's truth to its own safe-keeping, eliminates all doubt in this possession of the truth and punishes all deviation from it with excommunication. It lies in that religious fanaticism which identifies its own cause with God's cause and condemns as demonic all that runs counter to its own cause.

It is this one attitude which finds concentrated expression in Christianity's claim to absoluteness. Wherever Christians used violence against those of other faiths, it was this claim which gave them justification. It presented itself, and still presents itself, as the supreme expression of firmness and steadfastness in faith, and yet in reality is a travesty of this faith, which deeply contradicts its nature, instrumentalizes it and misuses it.

But we must not make things too easy for ourselves and attribute the absolutizing of Christian faith wholly to an alien principle which has taken possession of it and turned it into its opposite – like megalomania or an obsession with power. It has roots in the faith itself, which after all imposes an unconditional obligation. But it does not necessarily stem from it. There are particular conditions which bring out such absolutism. And it is in the light of these conditions that the absolutizing is to be understood and judged: the claim to absoluteness does not sound the same from Crusaders as it does from persecuted Christians.

In this book I want to investigate such an absolutizing of Christian faith. I want to investigate the manifestations of the Christian claim to absoluteness, the conditions in which it arises and it develops. We shall not be examining it 'in itself', detached from the situations in which it appears, but in context.

It will prove to be a phenomenon with many aspects, which cannot be sweepingly condemned and eliminated from Christian faith. There are exceptional situations in which a claim to absoluteness is not only a legitimate but even a necessary expression of a steadfast confession. Or situations in which clear and unconditional stands are required, say against totalitarian regimes which wage wars of conquest, exterminate minorities and violate human rights. But there is a wide range of manifestations of the Christian claim to absoluteness between the extremes of 'absolutism in an emergency' and 'the absolutism of domination' mentioned above – the control, repression and oppression of others. The types of faith which we shall meet in the following chapters lie in the broad realm between megalomania, fanaticism and the courage to confess.

As I have already said, all forms of the Christian 'absolutism of domination' call for the sharpest repudiation, not just on the basis of the Enlightenment postulates of toleration, but also from the heart of Christian faith itself. I would apply to them – and only to them – what Karl Jaspers said about the Christian claim to absoluteness generally. 'Both in its motive and in its consequences this claim is a disaster for human beings. We must oppose this fatal claim for the sake of the truth and the sake of our our souls.'[5] For the view that God's salvation is reserved for those who belong to a particular religion is an 'abhorrent and repulsive self-righteous idea'.[6]

But I do not want to stop at repudiation. I also hope to show that the heart of Christian faith can give impetus to a dialogue with adherents of other religions.

After a first encounter with very different forms of radical Protestantism (Chapter 1) I shall move into the camp of the Evangelicals and Christian fundamentalists (Chapter 2). Here I find forms of faith and life in which traits of Christian 'absolutism' are manifest. Then (3) I shall attempt to bring these phenomena together in a typical picture of the 'absolutist' attitude and its spiritual foundations. The following chapters trace the different roots of this attitude, roots which lie in the structure of the human personality (4) and in the world in which we live (5). So in Chapter 4 I am concerned with a *psychological* approach to the topic and in Chapter 5 with more of a *sociological* one. Here the conditions emerge in which claims to religious absoluteness arise. In the history of Christianity there were quite often situations which forced individual believers or the faith community to defend themselves, as we shall see in Chapter 6. Particularly in the beginnings of

Christianity, such a defensive struggle against superior powers which were felt to be a threat to the existence of the community – first of all against Judaism, the mother religion of Christianity, and then against Hellenistic syncretism – produced sharp claims to absoluteness (Chapters 7 and 9). Thus the well-known passages in the Bible which have been and are constantly cited in support of these claims can be understood in terms of contemporary confrontations (8). Then the page turns: in the fourth century Christianity is elevated to become a state religion and the claim to sole validity which was hitherto advanced only by theology can now be backed up by state law (10). With the rise and threateningly rapid expansion of Islam, the attitude of Christianity became more radical to the point of providing a theological justification for the Crusades (11). The Reformers opposed their '*solus Christus*' ('through Christ alone') to all church triumphalism and in so doing justified the Protestant form of the Christian claim to absoluteness (12). Since to this point I shall have followed only the line of a sharp opposition of Christianity or the message of Christ to other religions, in Chapter 13 I shall outline a more positive, 'inclusive' attitude to the religions which, while not abandoning the claim to absoluteness, clearly opens it up. Only in the nineteenth century does the history of the concept of the 'absoluteness of Christianity' begin, and with it a whole new attempt – starting from comparative religion – to justify this claim (14). This trend prompts me to ask in what way Judaism and Islam, Hinduism and Buddhism define their relationship to the other religions in terms of their origins (15). And at the end of our journey I shall try to show how Christian faith not only allows a renunciation of claims to absoluteness and encounter with those of other faiths in dialogue, but even requires it (16).

Before I begin to trace Christianity's claim to absoluteness I must reflect briefly on this elusive concept, which is so difficult to grasp. For first of all it contains so many semantic fields that it is almost impossible to define comprehensively. And secondly, it derives from certain philosophical and theological roots and is bound up with the intellectual tradition which derives from them.

First, on closer inspection phrases which one can describe as claims to absoluteness are classified in a wealth of individual and very different claims to validity, for example in claims to uniqueness (singularity), to exclusiveness, to universality and finality, to unconditional obligation, completeness, infallibilty and unsurpassability. The selection and composition of these claims decides what the claim to absoluteness means on each occasion.

And secondly, quite evidently talk of the absoluteness of Christianity does not originate in the Bible. Its theological career began only at the beginning of the nineteenth century in connection with Schelling and Hegel, who had described Christianity as 'absolute religion'.

If we reflect on the degree to which talk of the absoluteness of Christianity is bound up with the philosophy of German idealism and its influence, we can understand why scepticism about this claim is predominant among theologians. For example, for H. Döring the consequence is 'that the theologian should use this formula with care, in order not to get involved in the many problems which have become associated with it in more recent intellectual history'.[7]

On the other hand, if we need one term to describe the Christian claims to sole validity or superiority in religion in a succinct and evocative way, then is there any more apt than 'absoluteness of Christianity'? In that case, of course, a distinction must be made between the scientific meaning of this term, which is to be understood against the background of its philosophical origin, and the everyday use of it. This is the sense in which I shall be talking about the 'absoluteness of Christianity' and the Christian claim to absoluteness. Here I am certainly not concerned with the problematical term as such, but with what it denotes.

So I am taking the liberty of using the term relatively independently of its intellectual history, in order to be able to employ it in an evocative and varied way without restrictions. I shall also use the terms 'absolutism' and 'absolute' in this way; it may be somewhat blurred, but it is full of meaning.

Let us now investigate the Christian claim to absoluteness in its Protestant form by means of three very different examples.

I

Radical Protestants – Three Examples

'Whether we like it or not, paradoxically the fundamentalist movement has become one of the main means of communicating and inculturating the Protestant form of Christian faith in today's world' (M.Volf).

1. In Central and South America today there is an 'offensive on the part of the fundamentalist evangelical sects'[1] (above all charismatic groups and the Pentecostal movement). Forty million people are now said to belong to fundamentalist Protestantism throughout Latin America, half of them in Brazil. In the last ten years the growth of this movement has assumed a dimension which 'far transcends the process of conversion during the Reformation in sixteenth-century Europe'.[2] It is a 'fundamentalism of the poor',[3] which opens up a direct approach to God for those who have been degraded to what Gutiérrez calls 'non-persons', independent of all church authorities, and thus gives them a new feeling of worth.

8000 fundamentalist missionaries are active in Guatemala alone, supported by North American parent organizations. Many of them combine religious indoctrination with an ultra-conservative political propaganda which calls for unconditional submission to the existing political power structure. Not a few of the missionaries collaborate with the secret police and the military. The extremists among them even take part in the persecution of Catholic and Protestant priests who do not join them. But it is above all the Indios who are brutally persecuted by being billetted in 'defensive villages', tortured and murdered. A preacher from the fundamentalist group El Verbo declared: 'The army does not massacre Indians. It massacres demons, and the Indians are possessed by demons; they are Communists.'[4]

2. In the United States, Christian fundamentalism has a tradition going back over more than a century. It arose towards the end of the

nineteenth century as a defensive movement against modernism, rationalism and secularism. In 1910–1915 a series of pamphlets appeared entitled 'The Fundamentals', which gave the movement its name. Five fundamental convictions were regarded as indispensable: 1. belief in the verbal inspiration of the Bible and thus its inerrancy; 2. the virgin birth; 3. the vicarious atoning sacrifice of Jesus on the cross; 4. the bodily resurrection; and 5. the imminent second coming of Christ.

After a varied history, towards the end of the 1970s and at the beginning of the 1980s fundamentalism grew much stronger. Since then it has succeeded in gaining a massive influence on politics. Three large organizations, Moral Majority, Christian Voice and Christian Roundtable, gave Ronald Reagan massive support in his election campaign, and their members were appointed to numerous political offices. The new Christian Right developed in close connection with the new political Right on the basis of economic neo-liberalism, social traditionalism and militant anti-Communism. 'Pro-life', 'pro-traditional family', 'pro-morality', 'pro-American' were and are the slogans.[5]

The 1978 Chicago Declaration on the Inerrancy of the Bible marked the start of this movement.[6] The Declaration states that the original text of the Bible is absolutely infallible and inerrant in all its statements. That also applies to the historical and scientific information it contains. To justify this view, reference is made to the absolute truthfulness of God. From this it follows conclusively that any word of God as contained in the Bible must be absolutely true. If one were to allow room for doubt about even one passage, nothing else in it would be certain.[7]

3. A great evangelical campaign took place in Essen, Germany, between 17 and 21 March 1993 and was broadcast by satellite to 1400 places in Europe. It was called 'ProChrist'.[8] 42,000 people in Essen, a million people throughout Germany, and about ten million in Europe heard the American Baptist Billy Graham preaching for five evenings. His sermons ended with an invitation to the audience to turn personally to Jesus, the only way to salvation. In contrast to 'classical' pietism, for which the social and charitable consequences of conversion were important, Graham shows primarily an interest in the saving of souls, individualist love of neighbour.

Once again I should point out quite clearly that these three examples are not all on the same level. The militant fundamentalist sects in Central and South America should not be lumped together with the North American fundamentalists who are striving for political influence in order to apply the gospel in society. And these in turn are different from the German evangelicals – though more politically than theologically. In Germany the Protestant communities are not so concerned with a consistent Christian shaping of society; rather (so far, at any rate), they are content with arousing individuals to faith, with evangelization in the broadest sense. Perhaps all these groups agree on only one thing: on the unshakable certainty that there is only one way to God – the way that they advocate. In propagating this way, they believe that they are fighting for God's cause; they are fighters who are zealous to bring about God's will radically, consistently and without compromise.

Now that we have made contact with groups which give a 'social form' to Christianity's claim to absoluteness I want to look more closely at the spiritual foundations of the evangelicals and Christian fundamentalists. What are their basic convictions? And what is the difference between evangelicals and fundamentalists? As we discuss this question, it is important to remember that the evangelical movement throughout Europe is strongly influenced by the North American evangelicals. So we may suppose that phenomena which can be noted in America will in due course also appear in Europe.

2

Evangelicalism and Protestant Fundamentalism

The influence of evangelicals is a wide one, and can be found in state institutions as well as in the church. One of the best known evangelicals in Germany is Peter Beyerhaus, who holds the Chair for Mission and Ecumenical Theology at the University of Tübingen. He describes the openness of many evangelical Christians to dialogue with non-Christian religions which has come about since the Third Assembly of the World Council of Churches in New Delhi in 1961 as 'post-Christian syncretism'. In his view, this syncretism is 'a sublimation of the age-old dramatic struggle between God and his satanic opponents for the rule of the world. In his Son Jesus Christ God has taken possession of the world and of humankind as his unlimited sphere of rule. Advancing the message of Christ means ridding this world of demons and dethroning the prince of this world [Satan]. That is why Satan attempts to weaken and take control of this message before his final annihilation, by persecuting the community from outside and by perverting it from within. He does not hesitate to use any means to achieve this goal.' Satan has the vision of a single universal church and religion 'in which there will be room for every confessional statement, every religious conviction, every ideological programme'. Here he succeeds in deceiving a large part of Christianity and leading it astray. 'The ultimate issue in this last triumph of syncretism will be whether the community of Jesus Christ called to martyrdom does or does not exist, and its annihilation will be prevented only by the return of Jesus Christ and its rapture to him (I Thess.4.17).'[1] Accordingly, any dialogue between the religions will take place on the spiritual basis of this 'post-Christian syncretism' and thus play into the hands of the Antichrist. Thus Beyerhaus can say that the whole dialogue programme of the WCC 'clearly has the character of Antichrist'.[2]

How this position is expressed specfically in connection with individual non-Christian religions can be studied in a statement on Islam which Beyerhaus participated in drafting: 'We recognize in Islam a judgment of God on a Christianity which has often distanced itself from the biblical gospel. But we also recognize in Islam a power of the Antichrist to lead people astray in the last days (I John 2.18, 22), which fights against both the Jews, the people of the old covenant, and the church of Jesus Christ. The danger it poses lies in its deceptive imitation of the biblical revelation. We therefore call upon all Christians to study Islam watchfully, to meet its adherents with a clear view of their gospel aims, and to oppose its errors in a spiritual readiness to defend themselves (Eph.6.10–17).[3]

The principles of the evangelical movement include the absolute claim that redemption and salvation for human beings have come about solely in Jesus Christ. Thus the Lausanne Declaration of 1974, which is still the binding document of the evangelical understanding of mission, states: 'There is only one Redeemer and only one gospel . . . We repudiate as a slight on Jesus Christ and the gospel any syncretism and any dialogue which claims that Jesus Christ speaks equally through all religions and ideologies. Jesus Christ, true man and true God, gave himself as the sole redemption for sinners. He is the only mediator between God and man. And there is no other name by which we are saved. All men and women are lost in their sin. But God loves everyone. He does not will that anyone should be lost, but that everyone should repent. However, those who reject Jesus Christ scorn the joy of salvation and thus condemn themselves to eternal separation from God' (section 3).

According to James Barr, 'evangelicalism' denotes a group among Christians, while 'fundamentalism' denotes an attitude of mind.[4] That is already evident from the fact that one can encounter fundamentalist attitudes in all confessions, religions and world views, whereas the evangelical movement cannot be detached from the Christian religion. So we can state that Christian fundamentalism is an attitude of mind which occurs in the evangelical movement and on its periphery leads to the formation of distinctive groups.

13

However, one cannot call the whole evangelical movement fundamentalist.

How do fundamentalists differ theologically from evangelicals? Basing himself on the analyses of Barr, Marquardt and Joest,[5] Friedhelm Jung first of all defines the basic theological positions which fundamentalist evangelicals share with non-fundamentalists, and then distinguishes the specifically fundamentalist convictions:[6]

Both fundamentalists and evangelicals

- regard Holy Scripture as the supreme authority for the doctrine and life of Christians;
- believe in the vicarious atoning sacrifice of Jesus Christ and his bodily resurrection from the dead;
- expect the visible return of Jesus Christ;
- emphasize conversion and personal faith in Jesus Christ as a condition of salvation from eternal damnation.

In addition, fundamentalists stand for:

- the verbal inspiration and consequently the infallibility and inerrancy of the Bible in all its statements in the original text;
- a strict rejection of modern theology (the historical-critical method);
- a tendency towards the conviction that Christians can have only quite specific political and economic views;
- a tendency to absolutize their own standpoint, with the result that in their eyes all those who think otherwise are not true Christians.

This last point makes it clear that the Christian claim to absoluteness in its blunt form as a claim that only its own standpoint of faith is valid is not characteristic of evangelical Christians as a whole but primarily only of the fundamentalist wing. In other words, evangelicals and fundamentalists differ not so much in the content of what they believe as in the way in which they deal with this content, in the way in which they understand their faith and present it to others.

This hypothesis can be confirmed in connection with the understanding of the Bible which is central to evangelical Christianity. For all evangelicals, 'the divine inspiration, authority and all-sufficiency of the Holy Scriptures' is absolutely certain.[7] But however much agreement there may be on the principle, views rapidly diverge when it comes to making these terms more precise. 'Does inspiration extend to the whole Bible in all its statements (verbal or total inspiration), or are only parts of the Bible inspired (say, just the theological statements)? Does inspiration mean the inerrancy of the Bible (in the original text) or must one take into consideration errors in the biblical texts? Does the authority of Holy Scripture hold in such an unqualified way for Christians of the twentieth century as it did for those of the early church?'[8]

Jung distinguishes two major lines within the evangelical understanding of scripture: moderate Reformation biblicism and strict fundamentalism.[9] The fundamentalists assert the inerrancy of the Bible in all its parts and reject any biblical criticism. By contrast the moderates follow Luther, who on the one hand defended his *sola scriptura* principle, but on the other could make quite critical remarks about biblical writings (like the Letter of James). In their view, therefore, the Bible is inerrant in all that is necessary for faith, i.e. in all its theological statements, but not, say, in statements relating to its picture of the world. This 'moderate' position can even approve of a careful application of historical-critical biblical exegesis. But as a rule the evangelicals set a historical-*biblical* method over against the historical-critical method.[10] For where God's revelation is concerned, they regard any form of human criticism as inappropriate.

But even when fundamentalist evangelicals assert the absolute inerrancy of the Bible, some of them make the qualification that this inerrancy does not apply to the text as we have it: the contradictions which it contains are too manifest. Rather, the inerrancy applies to an original text which is postulated (but is no longer extant). This first excludes the possibility that God could have made an error which was written down in the texts by mistake. And secondly, it allows for the possibility that discrepancies have crept in in the process of tradition.

Behind the difference between moderate and fundamentalist biblicists lie different answers to the question of the degree of brokenness in which the eternal Word of God has entered the human world. Has it taken on the ideological stamp of a particular culture at a particular time, or has it asserted itself in a sovereign way in the face of all historical conditions and influences? The method of interpretation decides the answer to this question. Are biblical texts to be understood outside the context in which they came into being, so that they have to be translated if they are to speak to another context, or have they a validity that transcends time, so that they are equally near to any time in an eternal present, and any attempt at transformation must result in falsification? Fundamentalist biblicists would give priority to this second answer.

James Barr has demonstrated that some modern Christian fundamentalists by no means practise a purely literal interpretation of the Bible.[11] In his view they absolutize not so much the wording of Holy Scripture as such, as the correctness, i.e. inerrancy, of the statements. The Bible contains direct, inerrant revelation from God which was written down without any human (e.g. cultural) influence, free from human opinions and verdicts, convictions and values. But the significance of the statements need not lie on the surface of what is said. So these Christian fundamentalists make classifications within the Bible, supplement and interpret where the wording endangers their faith in the pure divine nature of scripture. They do not interpret the Bible in a completely literal way, i.e. in faithfulness to the letter (which indeed, if applied consistently, would be a critical principle of interpretation – critical of their own conviction). Instead of this they make a distinction – governed by tacit presuppositions – between passages which are to be understood literally and passages which are not.

They apply a non-literal interpretation above all where the Bible contradicts assured insights of modern science, for example that the creation of the world is conceivable only over an extremely long span of time and not in a day or in a sequence of six days. Thus they interpret 'day' in the creation story as a symbolic expression, specifically in order to salvage the historical accuracy of the 'report' which is so important to them. In so doing they contradict the manifest intention of the authors of the creation narrative who, when they say 'day', mean day. We must take these statements literally if we want to understand them authentically, but we may not simply take them over. For they are to be explained from the circumstances of their time, as we shall see in the next chapter. We must recognize the sense of the statements and express them in a new and different way for our time – precisely in order to do them justice.

Christian fundamentalists also resort to a non-literal interpretation where they want to harmonize contradictions, for example the inconsistencies between the two creation narratives or between the descriptions of the course of Jesus' life in the four Gospels. Here is one of the many examples which Barr adduces. According to Genesis 21, Ishmael was a small child when Hagar was sent into the wilderness. But Genesis 17 relates that he was thirteen years old when Isaac was born. The simplest explanation, which takes both texts literally, is that they are to be assigned to two different sources. But there is nothing Christian fundamentalists abhor so much as historical-critical source criticism. For this criticism presupposes that the biblical texts are not to be regarded as the immediate and pure word of God but as human traditions of experiences with God at a particular time. So fundamentalists who are interested in the infallibility of the Bible must use every conceivable expedient to interpret away such inconsistencies. In so doing, however, they make the Bible laughable.

The well-known hostility to theology among fundamentalist evangelicals can be explained from this concern to safeguard the inerrancy and infallibility of their own interpretation of scripture. Their practice of Bible study also corresponds with this: individual verses (e.g. John 14.6) are time and again recited as the ultimate justification. Members of these groups often do not study the Bible themselves, but consult authoritative persons and allow themselves to be instructed by them.[12]

Biblicism or biblical positivism is a characteristic of Protestant evangelicalism – 'biblical' is the key word. On the Catholic side, it is more authoritarianism and dogmatism which play this central role: the 'absolutizing of particular traditions or statements of the papal magisterium without regard to the historical context in which they were made and with no sense of the hierarchy of individual truths'.[13]

The traditionalist defence of church authority is the form taken by this Catholic fundamentalism. Here the church makes the claim to give direction to social morality and politics in accordance with Christian principles (its principles! – integralism). This tendency is at present being expressed in a disturbing way in the theopolitical claims to power by the Catholic church in the states of the former Eastern block. Whereas Protestant fundamentalism tends to take shape 'from below', in opposition to the established churches, Catholic fundamentalism proceeds 'from above', from the higher echelons of the church's hierarchy. It becomes crystallized in and around communities like Opus Dei, Corpus Angelorum, the Peter Brotherhood, the Una Voce movement or the Priestly Brotherhood of St Pius X, created by Archbishop Marcel Lefebvre, who was later excommunicated.[14]

A remark by Paul Natterer, the Regent of Lefebvre's seminary for priests in Zaitzkofen, while not representative of the whole movement, is worth noting. He thinks that 'delicts against the faith are more serious than capital crimes. The Inquisition and a "possible death penalty" are conceivable in a "Christian order".'[15]

Common to both Protestant and Catholic versions is an ideological positivism. In other words, the foundation of faith to which fundamentalists appeal does not consist primarily in an open, living creative relationship to God but in 'objective' saving facts. In his revelation God has made known truths about these saving facts which are eternally valid once for all. And these truths are in turn set down in the Bible as the primal written expression of the Word of God, in dogmas and confessions of the church. Like the saving facts themselves, so too information about them is given beforehand, absolutely fixed and in this sense 'positive'. It exists for all time and does not need to be developed or justified for a particular present, but only proclaimed.

The immediate consequence of this is that in matters relating to our relationship to God there can be no open quest for truth or free decision, but only obedience to the authoritative revelation. This basic attitude further explains the ambivalent attitude of fundamentalists to modern science. While they reject everything that contradicts the biblical tradition, on the other hand they make use of all the opportunities offered by science to support the biblical statements. The Enlightenment which led to the emancipation of thought from the authority of the Christian tradition is sharply rejected. The Enlightenment which opens up ways in science and technology of supporting this authority and disseminating the message of Christ is welcome.

Thus Werner Gitt, professor of mathematics and director of a technological institute of physics, has applied all his skills in mathematics and physics to proving the 'correctness' of the biblical accounts – say of the creation or the flood. He comes to the conclusion that 'the biblical account of creation is divine information which bears the seal of absolute truth, as do all other parts of scripture. It is a factual account which has to be taken literally in every detail. It contains fundamental scientific facts which are an indispensable basic system for research, with results which are true to reality.'[16] In the details of his arguments it can be seen to what an extent highly developed technical reason can put itself at the service of an unenlightened irrationalism.

As we saw above, many Christian fundamentalists today go beyond such a rationalistic treatment of the Bible. But they do so with precisely the same intentions as that of Gitt, namely to prove the 'correctness' of biblical reports as historically circumstantial factual truth. Thus a burden of proof is placed on the Bible which it is not its purpose to bear. In the quest for 'objective' truth the living word of God is objectified.

Evangelicals and fundamentalists have an extremely positive attitude towards the achievements of technological process, as they do towards technological rationality, at any rate in so far as these achievements serve their own cause. North American funda-mentalists above all are well known for their use of the most modern means of communication. To further their cause, they have developed a process of focussed mailing, and they practise fund-raising and lobbying. But the focal point of all their activities is tele-evangelization, the suggestive effect of which is constantly heightened by research into its socio-psychological effectiveness. Dorothee Sölle describes how this system works. 'While the music plays and a prayer begins, the telephone number appears in-creasingly frequently on the screen. Anyone who calls in is caught up in the selling system. The electronic church is not only television, but a selling technique using television, telephone calls, letters and lists of addresses. Once one has received the free gift one is bombarded with letters and brochures. The "great need which can be met only by your own personal gift" is stated, and there is a stamped addressed envelope for the cheque. If nothing happens after two or three letters, the computer spits the name out again. If a donation is made, more letters come, their tone depending on the level of the gift, in a cream envelope for all those who give $500 or more ... Every call and every letter is answered personally. The scientifically tested method is perfect. Computers sort the mail into marriage, alcohol and other problems and write long personal letters, indistinguishable from real letters; the stamps are stuck on. Those who are attracted by the television broadcasts and dial the number are given advice and Bible sayings; their names and addresses go into the computer. Then later they receive a prayer list to mark: alcohol, anxiety states, arthritis, asthma ... a personal prayer from a voluntary helper for every problem from A to Z."[17]

At this point I shall break off my description of Christian fundamentalism. It was meant to show the social form in which Christianity's claim to absoluteness manifests itself. Here some insights are already opening up into the spiritual foundations of this view of Christianity. In the next chapter I want to go a step further, look more closely at these spiritual foundations and systematize them. In so doing I shall have to make some critical remarks.

The account will be more removed than it has been so far from the concrete reality of Christian fundamentalism in order to typify such an attitude. This approach depends on generalizations and is therefore always in danger of becoming a stereotype. That makes it vulnerable. So it is important for me to say in advance that the description will not fit all features of all fundamentalist groups, far less all evangelicals. My sole concern is to bring out the fundamental and central characteristics of Christian 'absolutism' and to make clear the connection between these characteristics.

This will be an outsider's perspective, which cannot do justice to the self-understanding of what is described. But this outsider's perspective does not set out to be dogmatic; it is ready to engage in dialogue with the perspectives of insiders.

3

Religious 'Absolutism' as an Attitude and a Pattern of Behaviour

Those who make absolute claims about their Christian faith are not simply making an intellectual assertion about truth. They are making a deeply committed existential confession for which they are claiming unconditional validity. They are not primarily giving information about a particular state of affairs, but bearing resolute witness which challenges anyone confronted with it to react. Christian claims to absoluteness are not uninvolved, neutral assessments, but proclamations, slogans with a high emotional content which are often polemical. This supreme expression of personal involvement and commitment can easily (but not necessarily) be combined with dissociations from forms of faith and life which are not Christian, or are Christian in another way, stating a position and a negation, affirming (endorsing one's own faith) and condemning (other convictions).

Those who make claims to absoluteness are not performing individual isolated speech-acts, but rather expressing a whole attitude which is as it were concentrated in this one speech-act in the utmost density. And this attitude, this type of religious feeling, is manifested not only in this indivvual speech-act but also in a whole complex of attitudes and modes of behaviour. So it can be said that a claim about the absoluteness of Christian faith stands less for the particular content of this faith than for a way of dealing with the content of faith. It denotes an attitude to the content of faith, a form of piety. I call this attitude the 'absolutist' attitude.

Similarities to such a way of dealing with Christian convictions can be found in other religions and world-views. So it has to be said that claims to absoluteness are not a characteristic of particular confessions, religions or world-views but belong to a whole syndrome of religious and ideological self-absolutizing which can occur in all confessions, religions or ideologies.

What Hans-Jürg Braun says about 'fundamentalists' can also be understood as a description of the 'absolutist' attitude: 'Fundamentalism can have any kind of content, and thus quite different contents. Religious, political, ethical and allegedly scientific content is possible. The content is made tabu, protected from rational analysis and advocated with (fanatical) zeal. And it is usually put forward with claims to absoluteness, so that learning processes which could raise questions . . . are impeded.'[1]

This already indicates some aspects of the 'absolutist' attitude.[2] They all have their basis in that 'absolutism about the truth' which is characterized by an unshakable insistence that one's own religion – or more precisely one's own view of that religion – has sole, exclusive and complete possession of the truth. It is removed from the flux of historical coming to be and passing away, elevated to a status of eternal and unchangeable validity, and protected against criticism and progress in knowledge. That explains the resistance to a free (scientific) quest for truth. The 'desire for certainty' wins out over the 'desire to know reality'.[3]

A particular view of biblical reality is categorized and fixed, protected from rational analysis and immunized against all questioning. The monopoly, tabus and isolation entailed here are justified above all by appeal to a direct divine revelation. Fundamentalism begins where convictions are absolutized, i.e. derived from ultimate truths which are held to be absolutely valid and behind which it is impossible to investigate. Critical thought has to stop at these ultimate truths. What is required of believers is not insight but submission. But a high price has to be paid for a certainty free of doubt, with one's own faith at the centre of the truth, at the navel of the world: a surrender of intellectual freedom.[4]

Ideological criticism regards claims to absoluteness as elements of strategies of immunization aimed at safeguarding the sole validity of this content, which is taken to be absolute by the attribution of uniqueness to it. They deny validity to all notions, moral ideas, patterns of life, views of the world, institutions which are potential rivals, in order to deny any competition from the start.

Faith, which first and foremost is an attitude of open trust, is consolidated into a closed system of absolute facts: rigid orthodoxy instead of creative originality in appropriating tradition. Personal conviction about the liberating force contained in the message of Jesus Christ becomes a rigid 'I'm right'. And that is not the way in which Martin Luther or the Pietists or John XXIII or the first Christians believed. That is what they fought against.

In addition there is a claim to universal validity (in time and space). A claim to the totality of the revelation underlying one's own faith becomes a totalitarian claim about the interpretation of the world and the aims and goals of all people at all times. The consciousness of mission, of possessing a message of salvation for all people, becomes a more or less fanatical zeal for propaganda and conversion.

Those who advocate their conviction in an 'absolutist' attitude will present this conviction not as their view of the truth but as a direct description of the truth as fixed reality. They will not say, 'I see it in this way', 'I believe', 'I am convinced . . .', but 'It's like this – in this way and no other.'

There are no epistemological problems – in respect either of the reality of the world or of the reality of God. For God, who is a God of truth, has clearly disclosed his nature and his will, the truth about human beings and the world, present and future, heaven and earth, in Holy Scripture. Martin E. Marty, one of the most significant researchers into fundamentalism, aptly describes such rationalism as 'anti-hermeneutical'.[5]

According to this naively realistic understanding of truth, truth means correct information about things in earth and heaven: truth about the facts which is allegedly proved by the way in which it corresponds to the situation which it expresses. The Bible becomes a 'storehouse of facts' from which a 'theology of facts' is developed.[6] This is the positivist nineteenth-century scientific concept of truth which contemporary scientific thought has long superseded. The biblical tradition, with its quite different view of truth, is painted over.[7] I shall be describing this biblical understanding of truth in Chapter 16.

Now where the biblical tradition is pressed into the scheme of factual truths, we find what Paul Watzlawick calls the 'confusion of first- and second-order realities'.[8] The 'first-order reality' is the world of facts; the 'second-order reality' begins where meaning, significance and value is attributed to facts. There is objectivity and certain knowledge only in 'first-order reality'; here it is the case that there can only be one truth, what *is*. By contrast, 'second-order reality' is always (necessarily) ambiguous; in other words, different significances stand side by side without being mutually exclusive. There is certainty here, but no absolutely sure knowledge. It is senseless to argue about who is right and who is wrong. However, it does make sense to argue about what significance is appropriate to a situation or even a text which offers proof or support.

Christian 'absolutists' will not see that talk about God is a different kind of language from the description of reality as disclosed to everyday experience; that religious symbols have many levels; and that their significance does not lie on the surface – that readers approach the Bible with a particular pre-understanding (shaped by their culture).

The truth is one. Since it is manifest, in their view there can be no pluralism of different perspectives on the truth, far less any pluralism of different truths. And if everything in the Bible is equally God's word, then there cannot be different levels or hierarchies of truth either. Instead of pluralism there is unity.

Anything that contradicts revealed 'objective' truth can only be untruth. If, for example, the theory of evolution does not correspond with the biblical account of creation, it can only be false because this account of creation is true. There is a failure to see that here two kinds of truth are being compared, which cannot be rivals because they are on different levels. The creation stories certainly do not seek to explain the origin of the world. They came into being from an experience of chaos at the time of their composition and seek to demonstrate, for their time as for any other, that there is a fundamental order in the world. They do not seek to explain the world but to disclose it.

This already identifies the next characteristic of the 'absolutist' attitude: dualism. Not only the knowledge of reality but reality itself is reduced to a simple, dual, black and white pattern: true and false, Christian and anti-Christian, believing and pagan, saved and lost. Humanity is divided into these two sides. Anyone who is not on the side of the one and only truth must be opposed to it, and therefore has to be fought against. Disparaging pre-judgments and generalizations about others – 'materialists', 'Muslims', 'lukewarm nominal Christians' – prevail. Open communication with them is no longer possible. Once the fronts have hardened, there are attributions of blame, accusations of treachery and conspiracy theories. Reality is then perceived increasingly markedly in clichés and stereotypes. Those of other faiths appear as the prefabricated hostile stereotype portrays them: not as individual persons, but as members of a group which is possessed by demonic error. Nothing is more remote than an attempt to understand them. A compulsion towards hostility prevails.

There is only the alternative of accepting or rejecting the sole way of salvation. The quest for middle ways or the recognition of several ways of being in the truth is already regarded as apostasy from the truth. Those with an 'absolutist' attitude see the plurality of religious convictions as a temptation to be resisted and one which tests their faith. There can never be a social consensus which decides on the truth: it is no coincidence that an anti-democratic attitude is the basic feature of any religious radicalism.

So the 'absolutism of truth' within is matched by a resolute defence against 'outsiders'. This can be expressed with different degrees of aggressiveness, from unreflecting resentment about the intellectual challenge posed by another's claim to truth to violent attacks on the existence of the other.[9] This is precisely the same structure as can be observed in xenophobia, with the difference that it is directed not against the ethnic but against the religious alien: the awareness of belonging to a particular religion is combined with the exclusion of other forms of faith and their adherents. Self-definition is achieved through the repudiation of others.

The dualistic 'positivism of facts' which I have described is usually combined with an equally dualistic 'legal positivism': 'The divine revelation contains not only facts but also commands, divinely sanctioned legal norms to which unconditional validity is attached. They are not only made directly binding without heed to historical and cultural conditioning but are also developed into a large-scale biblical system of norms of behaviour in which modern problems like abortion or Aids are given a clear place.'[10] Theological regimentation is matched by moral regimentation.

So in all probability a moral rigorism will be found within fundamentalist communities. Striving for perfect and pure truth is matched by striving for perfection and unsullied purity in individual lives and in the life of society. The obverse of this quest for perfection is a constant feeling of guilt, the feeling of not being able to do justice to the demands. But such a guilt feeling contains an aggressiveness directed inwards which can also easily be turned outwards – against others. Thus the striving for purity and perfection in faith and life becomes a yoke of tyranny for others.

Like missionary disputatiousness directed outwards, the control of faith and behaviour directed inwards is an immediate outcome of the claim to absoluteness. For those who are convinced that their faith is absolutely right and who feel called to help this faith to prevail, the end justifies the means.

One can even go a step further and make connections between Christian fundamentalism on the one hand and racist antisemitic and extremist right-wing tendencies on the other. In empirical investigations, studies on peace, prejudice and ideology at the end of the 1960s and beginning of the 1970s demonstrated a clear connection between a strictly orthodox, fundamentalist religion and an authoritarian, militaristic attitude. They called this connection the 'orthodoxy-militarism complex'. A punitive attitude (strictness) is one of the essential characteristics of this complex.[11] In religion it appears as strict orthodoxy.

So there is a close affinity between the absolutized religious attitude and the absolutized political attitude. Those with a basic fundamentalist attitude are far more prepared to justify the use of violence in conflicts with people who think differently than those who are basically prepared to engage in dialogue. 'Fundamentalism in principle does not exclude psychological and physical force as a means of establishing its claim to truth. The stubbornness of those who "deny" the truth, who oppose it, is to be combated by every possible means.'[12]

The 'absolutist' attitude immediately brings out a particular pattern of relationship in dealing with others. Anyone with this attitude who meets someone of another faith may formally maintain a relationship but in principle break it off by transforming it into a one-sided monological relationship, thus contradicting the nature of true relationships. This is then not a relationship between partners who in principle have equal rights, one which rests on the basic ethical law of mutuality. It is not an unmotivated acceptance of the other, but a strategic interaction aimed at self-assertion against the other. The other's convictions are rejected with a view to establishing the sole validity or at least superiority of one's own. Confrontation is unavoidable. Where the other does not submit, the relationship is put to a hard test. It is more likely to break down under the 'absolutist' attitude than to be able to break up this attitude. For those who adopt this attitude, truth – *their* truth – is more important than love. Their religious pleasure in themselves ultimately reflects a narcissistic self-love. 'Those who claim absoluteness in the name of the one God reflect themselves, and project themselves on God.'[13]

The dialogical attitude is diametrically opposed to the 'absolutist' attitude: here the basic movement is towards being open to others and their faith, not shutting oneself off, isolating oneself and barricading oneself in. This attitude consists in making room for the belief of the other, i.e. granting the other not only the right to exist but also a capacity for the truth and even knowledge of the truth. Those who adopt it must have the readiness and the sovereignty to transcend themselves, to come out of themselves in order to discuss with others. That makes them vulnerable. Dialogue involves a self-emptying, without giving up oneself and one's own claim to truth. I think that the aptest description of a dialogical attitude is in Paul, in I Corinthians 13.4–6.

This black and white portrait should not be misunderstood: there are many shades of grey between the absolutist and the dialogical attitudes. Moreover the attitudes described are not characteristics that people have, but attitudes which they adopt. Just as they can be adopted in certain circumstances, so too they can be dropped. But we shall see later that they can harden into what amount to characteristics.

This description of the absolutist attitude raises the question of the roots and the presuppositions of this attitude and the circumstances in which it arises. What brings it out? An answer to this question would help towards explaining and understanding the attitude. I can find such roots in three spheres: in Christian faith itself (as in any religion), in the world in which people live, and in particular personality structures.

In Chapter 15 we shall see that it is of the nature of any religion to make an unconditional claim to truth which puts an absolute obligation on its adherents. This claim does not relate to the religion itself but to its message, which is derived directly from the divine ground of all being and is aimed at leading to an encounter with this ground. Those who with absolute certainty trust in the presence of God in the sources of their own religion need not necessarily adopt the 'absolutist' attitude and declare all other religions worthless. But in certain conditions the unconditional claim to the truth of its message made by a religion can be a claim to absoluteness which declares belief in this message to be the sole and exclusive way to salvation for all men and women and sharply condemns convictions which are not in conformity with this.

Whether this limit is passed also depends – not least – on factors which do not lie in the religion itself: on presuppositions which arise from a particular situation or are present in the personality structures of individual believers. 'Inner' dispositions of character can be identified which make people prone to adopt an absolutist attitude. And there are external conditions, arising out of the situation, which prompt or encourage this attitude – circumstances which exert pressure and provoke resistance. The need for unconditional certainty about the truth which derives from the presence of God in religion may be matched by the disposition of a particular personality and a threatening situation (or one that is felt to be threatening) outside, so that the disposition becomes an attitude and the attitude a form of behaviour. But of course – and this need hardly be said – this does not happen automatically. Even if a whole series of such religious, psychological and situational risk-factors coincide, an absolutist attitude need not necessarily develop. So I prefer to talk about the roots rather than the causes of this attitude.

First of all we must consider the question what psychological dispositions lead people to adopt absolutist attitudes. In the following reflections I am not concerned simply with reducing the phenomenon of religious claims to absoluteness to psychological considerations or even with dismissing them as pathological. The psychological approach helps to bring out aspects of a complex phenomenon without being either able or willing to explain the phenomenon as a whole. The demonstration of personality types and individual stages is complicated, because it can be misunderstood as an arrogant categorization of people. Hence the remark that in what follows I am concerned with explaining attitudes and modes of behaviour through psychological models, not with labelling people or even engaging in pathology. I have no intention of labelling, stigmatizing and thus marking off a particular group. Rather, I want to show how the absolutist attitude grows out of quite normal dispositions of the kind that we all have within us.

4

The Claim to Absoluteness – Support
for the Self in Inner Uncertainty

'For the simple, religion itself becomes a substitute religion' (Max Horkheimer and T. W.Adorno)

In a psychological perspective, claims to religious absoluteness look
like strategies for coping with existential anxiety and spiritual
uncertainty: they function to reinforce the self in identity crises.

Three possible catalysts for this anxiety can be identified:

1. The enormous variety and complexity of reality gives rise to the
feeling of getting lost in the chaos of relativity. The basic feeling of
many people at present is that of leading a life in transition, a life in
the expectation of constant possible change in a notoriously restless
time, with no external guidance by binding traditions, no permanent
involvement in adequate, stable social systems, no underlying
meaning that they can take for granted. The risk of personal and
social crises is great, and the safety net is thin. Religious interpreta-
tions of life capable of offering metaphysically guaranteed certainty
in times of uncertainty have themselves got caught up in an identity
crisis: they are suffering a loss of credibility. The churches are in
search of a role in our changing society, so it is no wonder that in its
uncertainty over orientation, society expects less and less of them.

2. Our historical consciousness compels us to the insight that
everything, including the truths of faith which were once so firm, is the
product of historical developments; to the insight that truth has a
temporal core and is to be understood in terms of particular cultural
conditions; in short, to the insight that the truth – all truth – is exposed
to human influence. Where this historical consciousness finds its way
into theology, as in the historical-critical interpretation of the Bible,
for many Christians it can gnaw away at the certainty of their faith.

3. In addition there is the experience of religious plurality which we have every day in our multicultural society. Does not the multiplicity of religious convictions and forms of life contradict the truth-claim of individual convictions and forms of life?

All this can lead to the shaking of convictions which were believed to be unshakable, to the 'shock of relativity'. The feeling arises that everything could also be different; perhaps in the end only the chance of birth is responsible for my being a Christian and not a Muslim. This is the feeling that the ground is beginning to quake under our feet and that we have no firm place to stand, a feeling of uncertainty which gives rise to anxiety – spiritual, existential anxiety. Those who are thus driven out of their ancestral faiths have basically three possible ways of reacting to such religious homelessness.

First, with regression and withdrawal into a defensive position, with a refusal to engage in any discussion and a stubborn retreat into the once safe fortress. Such people stick their heads in the sand, deny the uncertainty and in compulsive repression hold on rigidly to their previous pattern of faith.

Secondly, with a militant counter-attack, with a monological stabilization of their own position, in which assertion upon assertion are cited in their support. Certainly they perceive the threat and deliberately react to it, but with a confessorial assurance, perhaps adopting the motto 'The Bible was right after all'. But this is a rearguard action in which an attack with the bludgeon of accumulated arguments is chosen as the best form of defence.

Thirdly and finally, in open dialogue with the challenges, thus incurring the danger that their own faith perspective may be changed and extended. However, this attitude presupposes a sovereignty and readiness for change which lives by the primal trust that to change one's own faith is not to lapse from faith but represents growth into a more comprehensive and richer faith. The creative power of constructive self-criticism widens horizons, and a new and more comprehensive awareness develops.

The first strategy is characteristic of a reactionary traditionalism which holds firm to the 'pre-revolutionary' state of what it supposes always to have been the case and buries itself in this retrospective utopia. One could also call this attitude of refusal rejectionism.

The second strategy is that of fundamentalism, which does not withdraw but takes the offensive by opposing its conviction, as God's irrevocable truth, to the resistance of the spirit of the age. That here it hardens into a dogmatic sense of being right and is associated with increasingly narrow claims to validity is seen by fundamentalists as an expression of the defensive power which lies in this truth. Traditionalism is the passive defensive side and fundamentalism the active offensive side of the absolutist attitude. Whereas fundamentalists engage in shaping the world, rejectionists tend more to cultivate their own religious life. Whereas the reactionary traditionalists deny modernity, fundamentalism represents 'a very modern reaction to modernity'.[1]

Finally, the third strategy is to be found wherever an authentic dialogue is sought with those of other faiths. Two things go with it: standing in and on one's own faith, and a recognition of the ultimate relativity of this or any faith in the face of the mystery of God which no human faith can grasp completely. This distinction between one's own assurance of truth and the truth of God which is beyond our control, a distinction which at the same time supports and relativizes one's own certainty, gives openness and ease in dealings with those of other faiths.

The difference between the three strategies can be seen clearly in the way in which they deal with criticism. Reactionary traditionalists take criticism as a confirmation of their prejudices about the critics. Fundamentalists react with a vigorous refutation or counter-criticism. The 'dialoguers' really accept criticism and grapple with it in order to accept its justified concern and to contradict objections which seem to be unjustified.

Which of these three strategies is chosen by those who are uncertain in their faith depends not least on their psychological dispositions. In his book *Basic Forms of Anxiety*,[2] Fritz Riemann has distinguished four fundamental personality structures which coincide with four characteristic anxieties, his 'basic forms of anxiety'. We all have these four tendencies within us to different degrees as perfectly normal reactions to challenges that we face in life. But where the balance between them is lost and one of them becomes dominant, pathological distortions develop, leading to the four major forms of neurosis. Riemann names his personality types after these.

The one-sidedly *schizoid* personality shrinks from inter-personal relationships and ties because it is afraid of becoming dependent on someone else and thus losing its own freedom and ultimately its self. Ideas, truths, principles seem more certain than human relationships, and unshakable religious principles more certain than open trust in a God who always keeps showing himself anew and then hiding himself again. Thus the lack of a capacity for relationship determines both one's relationship to others and one's relationship to God: truth comes before love, commitment to creeds before commitment to persons, even the 'person' of God.[3]

The one-sidedly *depressive* person becomes anxious in precisely the opposite way, afraid of becoming a real self. Such people are anxious about autonomy, isolation and loneliness and therefore seek security in surrender to others, to the extent of total symbiosis.

The one-sidedly *compulsive* personality experiences changes and alterations as uncertainty; it clings intensively, even tenaciously, to what exists, assuring itself by ordinances, doctrines and dogmas. Literalism, dogmatism and legalism could be the consequence.

The one-sidedly hysterical personality is afraid of precisely these factors, of finality and a lack of freedom; it is out for constant change.

Where the schizoid and compulsive elements of the personality structure have won through over the depressive and hysterical ones, the 'absolutist' attitude finds good conditions for growth. In the face of the disquieting plurality of reality, truths and values, it escapes into egocentric (or group-egocentric) isolation. To avoid the terror of 'everything is in flux', this type takes refuge in the sure home of the claim to absoluteness. A tense clinging to simple and irrevocable values and truths, to unproblematical and uniform rules and ordinances, to a stable foundation, becomes the backbone of its self-definition. In a cast-iron and unswerving way it holds fast to its view of faith in the face of all attacks. And in order to remove itself from the flow of time, from change and transitoriness, it elevates itself to become an eternally valid sacrosanct principle and encounters all strangers and others who could put in question its own claims to sole validity with mistrust and abhorrence. In the effort to find a firm support for a truth which is valid once and for all, which opposes all plurality like a rock in the breakers, faith is domesticated in formulae and doctrines and thus idolized. Compulsive self-assurance by separation from others in the attitude of 'thus and not otherwise', to keep away anything that is disquieting – that is a summary of the psychological view of the 'absolutist' defensive attitude that I have described.

An interesting supplement to this psychological model can be found in a comparison between the static system of co-ordinates in the four personality profiles as developed by Riemann and Fowler's dynamic model of psychological development. James W. Fowler describes the development of religious faith as a process which goes by stages, reaching the full form worth striving for in seven steps.[4]

I shall begin straight away with the third stage of 'mythical-verbal belief', characteristic of six- to ten-year olds. Religious symbols are interpreted literally. Their significance does not lie *behind* them but *in* them, does not lie in a deeper dimension, but on the surface of specific experience. It is felt, but not reflected on. At the fourth stage, this reified attitude of faith gives way to a personal bond to an authoritative person, a 'model'.

What is decisive for our theme is the transition from the pre-critical to the critical phase which begins at the fifth stage. Elements of faith which were previously accepted tacitly are questioned, demythologized and reformulated. The I detaches itself from outside guidance and strives for self-authorization. With increasing detachment from itself and from 'models', the third-person perspective develops. This transition from the fourth to the fifth stage is experienced as a crisis of faith. If it can be assimilated, then the I can also grow beyond the fifth stage. At the sixth stage, rival perspectives can be accepted without danger to the substance of one's own faith. For the believer has become aware that the divine reality does not lie in the religious traditions but is merely communicated by them. The fact that the religious symbols, traditions and forms of life can be seen only as incomplete, particular and limited in no way diminishes their value. In the attempt to grasp the many layers of reality, symbolic, mythical, poetic and metaphorical expressions gain new relevance. In this phase of a 'second naivety' there is a remythologizing of faith. An open dialogue with other experiences, claims to truth and religious traditions becomes possible in a mutual recognition of different ways of believing.

Fowler's line of development culminates in the seventh stage, the 'universalizing faith' in which the self empties itself in God, where it encounters the other, the stranger, as brother and sister.

This sequence of stages describes a process of increasing decentring and extension of perspectives: in its naive egocentricity the child knows nothing but its own perspective. Then it takes note of the mere existence of other perspectives, in order at the next stage to develop the capacity to adopt different perspectives. Young people acquire the third-person perspective and then learn as young adults to accept the irreconcilable plurality of perspectives in a kind of universal perspective.

This process can also be described as a way from a self-sufficiency which relates everything to itself to the capacity to empty oneself in the mutuality of dialogue.

Where it proves impossible to move from stage three to stage five, and where there is stagnation or even regression, the hardening of faith into claims to absoluteness can be the consequence. The lack of outside direction is then compensated for by a rigid internal direction.

Here, too, it is the assimilation of the experience of plurality which decides everything. The thought that everything could also be different, which grows out of the experience of the plurality of religions and world views, breaks open the safe confines of childhood belief and thus sparks off an identity crisis. This experience can set in motion a process of growth which makes faith broader and more open. But it can also lead to a denial of the threat and to withdrawal into a bastion which has long fallen.

In this second instance, faith and doubt, certainty and 'tribulation', are not integrated in the identity of faith. Rather, doubt is banished, projected outside, and faith is thus elevated to become a supposedly unendangered certainty. The claim to absoluteness compensates for the uncertainty in the self; here it is not those who fight against their uncertainty who tend to absolutize but those who cannot accept their own uncertainty and flee from it.

Jung once said that fanaticism is the brother of doubt. Where faith and doubt are torn apart, and where one's own doubt is projected on others, on unbelievers, fanaticism is not far off: being possessed by a truth which suppresses and fights against all that does not correspond to it.

5

The Claim to Absoluteness – A Spiritual Refuge in Outward Uncertainty

The previous chapter was concerned with those dispositions towards the shaping of the 'absolutist' attitude which lie within, in the person: weakness in the self and defects in maturity. We now turn to the 'external' risk factors, those which lie not within the individual, but in his or her political and economic circumstances, and also in the spirit of the age and social culture.

In the last chapter we already came up against some such factors: religious pluralism, an awareness of the historicity of all truth, and the impossible complexity of reality in our society. The constantly increasing differentiation in living conditions gives many people a sense of inability to get their bearing, a loss of orientation, so that they feel unable to cope. The stress that this produces leads to reactions of self-defence: the quest for a solid standpoint and a clear ordering principle on the basis of which it is possible to look over and through the impossibly complex situation and thus control it (at least intellectually).

Many people suffer from a loss of spiritual roots. In their eyes Western culture, which has been secularized and put in religious parcels, is suffering a loss of moral values and a dilution of religous belief. The longing arises for values which resist the transvaluation of values; there is a quest for truths which have unconditional and lasting validity in the maelstrom of a relativity which snatches everything into itself. Thus uncertainty makes people receptive to the offer of absolutely unshakable moral and spiritual values.

The best explanation for the fact that in the last few years 8000 German women not married to Muslim husbands have converted voluntarily to Islam is a quest for fixed rules in the morass of a progressive loss of meaning.

36

Order, orientation and meaning are closely connected. Where the order which previously supported them collapses – for example in the life of an individual (through a stroke of fate) or in the consciousness of an era (as after the Lisbon earthquake of 1755) – there is a deficit of meaning, and the quest for new meaning begins. The disappointment of great hopes can also lead to a cultural loss of meaning: hope for progress; hope for a scientific explanation of the world and technical mastery of the world or for psychoanalysis elevated to the status of a saving doctrine; hope also for the realization of a classless society. And a life of abundance which becomes satiety can also lead to an individual loss of meaning because it is felt to be a void without direction or aim: a life which has everything to live from but nothing to live for. The assurance of meaning and order in the life of the individual and the cultural community is an indispensable foundation for life.

Of course spiritual and existential uncertainty is markedly dependent on individual experience. For example, the religious pluralism which some people experience as an interesting enrichment seems to others to put their own faith in question. So it has to be said that the danger does not lie in pluralism and historicity as such, but in a particular way of experiencing this pluralism and historicity. The danger lies not so much in the external situation itself as in the way in which this situation is experienced. And this experience is in turn markedly dependent on dispositions of personality, as we saw in the previous chapter. However, it also depends on the cultural spirit of an age, which forms the intersubjective matrix of the subjective experience.

I want to demonstrate this with reference to Protestant belief in its century of orthodoxy. Here one can observe the connection between the shaking of the intellectual (and social) foundations of a whole culture and the consolidation of faith which was a response to this. It also emerges that spiritual anxiety about existence is by no means a phenomenon limited to our time. We meet it in the history of Christianity wherever there are crises of cultural identity as a result of global epoch-making revolutions.

After the shock caused by Copernicus and Bruno, people in the seventeenth century found themselves flung out of their global house, which had stood at the centre of creation and had been comfortable because it was finite and well ordered by God's hand. Now it was suddenly wandering like an isolated particle of dust through an endless universe – like an outcast, without a centre and lost. The optimism, the confidence in the harmony of the world and human beings, which had predominated in Renaissance humanism gave way to 'baroque pessimism'. Anxiety about the world, cosmic nihilism, a lament over meaningless because existence had fallen victim to death in a transitory world, governed the feelings of the age. W.Philipp called this sense of depression the 'world-frost of infinity'.[1]

'The theology of high orthodoxy is *threatened* theology. It feels its essence and existence attacked and put in question.'[2] And so it reacted above all with the strategy described in Chapter 4, i.e. defensively, by fighting a rearguard action, with dogmatic and confessional rearmament to safeguard the old picture of the world. It ensconced itself in a conservative biblicism which accumulated isolated biblical quotations, surrounded them with an aura of infallibility, and combined them with philosophical conceptual instruments into a fixed system of faith. Above all the doctrine of verbal inspiration was used as a support for this system and developed in a way alien to the Reformers.[3] The working of God's Spirit was objectified in the idea that inspiration had taken place only in God's dictation of the Bible – a historical event which had happened at a particular time in the past.

The church was perceived as being engaged in battle against the realm of the devil. This battle was being fought against all those into whom the devil had entered, against Turks, heretics and confessional opponents (this was the time of the Thirty Years' War). As Philipp writes, evidently the 'rabidly disputatious theology of the much-vaunted "century of orthodoxy" was "certain" of its own assailed faith, now attacked and put in question, only in the fight of all against all'.[4]

An ecclesiastical and theological absolutism developed in parallel to the political absolutism. The shaking of the world-view which had previously supported it had prompted this. A faith which had been shaken to the foundations sought refuge under a substitute metaphysical heaven. And the church which was inwardly so uncertain surrounded itself with external pomp, as is documented by the pompous cupolas of the time and the splendour of the interiors, bedecked with gold.

Alongside such experiences of spiritual and cultural threat there were even more massive dangers to the individual existence of individuals or the collective existence of whole groups: situations of material need and impoverishment, situations of social uprooting and political domination, situations of oppression and persecution.

Research into fundamentalism has shown that danger to the foundations of material, social and political life encourages a tendency towards religious radicalism. Fundamentalism comes into being where the foundations are tottering. It is an attempt to create new spiritual, social and political foundations which cannot be shaken.

The movements for re-Islamicization indicate how social, political and economic crises lead to radical religious movements among those concerned. The violation of individual and collective feelings of worth caused by such crises plays an important role here.

If we remember the degree to which the colonial domination of the 'Christian' West over the Islamic countries sparked off a feeling of economic, political, cultural and religious humiliation there, it is no wonder that in Iran, Shi'ite Islam understands itself as a liberation movement.[5] The revival of Islam which we are currently experiencing is not least a reaction to the humiliation of the Arab and Islamic feeling of worth. It is an attempt to restore the Islamic order of life and thus to anticipate the world along the way of religious renewal. The humiliation that has been suffered is being compensated for by a proud consciousness of mission.

Another form of humiliation which makes many people hope for the success of the re-Islamicization movement stems from living conditions in the countries themselves.[6] Whole classes live in degrading conditions, have often suffered economic and social decline, and have largely been excluded from the political process. In the North African states the Islamic fundamentalists find their following in the poor settlements of the big cities to which the former country population have migrated, disappointed in their hope of a better life in the city. A flight from the land, social uprooting, disintegration, a state of homelessness between modernity and tradition, determine their situation. The activists of the movement include college graduates who are unemployed and have no hope of a profession. They feel dependent, powerless and exposed. Both groups lack any foundation for their existence. They hope that a return to Islamic principles will improve their situation. And often Islamic renewal groups (like the Muslim Brethren in Egypt) in fact show considerable social commitment.

Re-Islamicization should not be over-hastily identified with fundamentalism: rather, fundamentalist Muslims are using the efforts towards a more religious Islamic renewal for their strongly political interests. They want to make the Sharia, i.e. the Islamic legal order as they understand it, binding on the whole state. Islam is 'a purely political and cultural counter-tendency which sets itself against alien cultural imperialism and strives for self-realization among the masses of the Muslim people'.[7] Here it can be seen that there is a close connection between national and religious reflection on one's roots – not only in Islam but in all religions. Nationalism and religious fundamentalism are related to each other.

Now if against this background we ask whether there are any comparable phenomena in Western countries which prompt a more radical religious attitude, we discover very much the same thing. Here too there is social uprooting and disintegration of the kind caused, say, by social mobility and the anonymity of the big cities. The North American fundamentalist groups find most of their new members among new arrivals, i.e. among people who have not yet put down social roots.[8] Here too social insecurity prevails.

Where economic decline endangers the previous standard of living, there is a sense of going downhill and being unable to prevent the decline. This economic insecurity can lead directly to social disintegration, for example where jobs or homes are lost. And social uprooting often leads to spiritual uprooting. So we can also understand fundamentalism as an attempt to replace torn up 'natural roots' with new 'artificial' roots.

The worldwide effects of modern industrial civilization which have led to dramatic aberrations that are endangering social survival are even less under the control of individuals (and therefore all the more worrying): the global destruction of the material foundations of life as a result of the pollution of the environment and the remorseless exploitation of natural resources and sources of energy, the waste of which conjures up threatening changes in climate; the flows of migration caused by the economic impoverishment of whole areas of the world, which spark off fears of chaos in Western countries in the face of the flood that is supposed to be on the point of breaking in; the tremendous potential for military annihilation which can easily get out of control; the ever-increasing overpopulation of the earth, and so on. All these tendencies make up a gloomy picture of the future which among many of our contemporaries creates a sense of facing the end of the world.

This mood makes people receptive to apocalyptic prophecies of the kind disseminated by evangelical and fundamentalist groups. Such groups increase and intensify anxieties and guilt-feelings by announcing an imminent and inevitable end of the world. This is said to be part of God's plan of salvation which will lead through judgment to the kingdom of God – but only for those who now decide for this true and saving way.

Such self-appointed prophets are certainly taking up biblical traditions, but they isolate them from other texts and detach them from their historical context in order to apply them directly to the present, with the hermeneutical simplicity described above, for which all times are equal. In other words, they absolutize these traditions.

In this way they are perhaps indeed able to banish anxiety about the future among their followers. The situation which is so terrifying at present appears as a dark vale of tears, at the end of which a new and glorious light will shine on those who have withstood the test. The certainty of belonging to these champions of God's cause gives that self-assurance which is important for survival – because it disarms helplessness. It gives meaning to the current situation and one's own suffering in it.

But how is the anxiety banished? By subordinating it to another even greater anxiety. Those who follow the apocalyptic prophets now fear not so much the prevalent chaos in the world as the 'woes of the end time' and the divine judgment which is imminent with the end of the world. For this is one of the characteristics of fundamentalist belief in God (in all the Abrahamic religions), which makes the God of love, mercy and forgiveness an accuser, judge and avenger.

Now if the fearful end of the world is the will of this God, not only does it make no sense to fight against the aberrations mentioned above; such a fight would even be a fight against God and thus sin. Social and political commitment to an improvement in living conditions would be an attempt to stop what may not be stopped. Because – according to this view – the splintering of humankind into hostile nations, religions and confessions is necessary, international organizations which seek to overcome it are ungodly. That leads to the well-known sharp criticism by such groups of the United Nations Organization and the ecumenical movement. The catastrophe for humankind must come, so that the time of salvation can dawn for the small flock of the redeemed. This is apocalyptic fatalism!

Now for an interim report. We have investigated 'external' conditions, factors in life which lead people to adopt 'absolutist' attitudes. In so doing we have come upon experiences of helplessness in situations of decline which lead to religious struggles for deliverance.

As a summary of what has been said, we can argue that religious claims to absoluteness arise from assimilating experiences of threat: where the material, social or spiritual foundations of existence cease to be supportive; where decay and disorder set in or seem to be setting in; where the religious and moral forces opposed to such decline are themselves drawn into the undertow of decadence. Religious claims to absoluteness arise where in self-defence against external uncertainty an even surer inner certainty is sought through direct divine assurance. Such claims are stabilizing factors, to provide support in conditions which have become unstable and where a world-view has been shaken. They are reactions to external pressure which – like physical pressure on a pliable mass – lead to inner consolidation in individuals and groups. So we may formulate the rule that external pressure on an individual or group leads to structures which exert spiritual or social compulsion on the individual or group.

But now we must go a stage further and envisage a different kind of emergency. This is the emergency which does not consist in spiritual uncertainty or in the social consequences of socioeconomic crises. What I mean is, rather, the emergency of Christians who are persecuted for their faith; the emergency of the church which is allowed no freedom of belief; the emergency of faith itself, which faces either being annexed to a dominant ideology or – where it fights against such an ideology – being exterminated. Here we come to know the claim to absoluteness advanced by Christian faith from another aspect, as an expression of ultimate resoluteness in resisting demonic absolutism. Here we meet what previously appeared as the totalitarian ideologizing of Christian faith in the form of a battle against totalitarian ideologies and systems.

6

The Claim to Absolute Truth –
A Bulwark in the Battle of Faith

Where Christian communities – and the same can be said of other religious faith communities – live as small minorities in the Diaspora, i.e. dispersed among those of another faith, isolated and dependent on themselves, or where they are even oppressed and terrorized by their hostile surroundings, they shut themselves off from the outside world and 'conspire' within to protect themselves and safeguard their identities. Because of the need to protect themselves which is forced upon them they withdraw to the nucleus of their faith, from which their power to resists stems – to the point of martydom. Here faith hardens into a bulwark, a protective wall against the persecutors; it assumes martial features and leads to very narrow, sharply exclusivist claims to truth.

There are numerous examples of such hostility to Christians – from the persecutions in the Roman Empire to the oppression in Iraq or south-eastern Turkey in our day. And one might recall the Church Struggle in the Third Reich from the most recent history of German Christianity.

In the Barmen Declaration, the 'Confessing Church' with Karl Barth as its theological spokesman opposed the National Socialist ideology (which itself could be called fundamentalist) and the assimilation of the German Christians to this ideology in the Barmen Declaration. The first thesis of this declaration contains a claim to exclusiveness: 'Jesus Christ . . . is the one Word of God whom we are to hear, whom we are to trust and obey in life and death. We repudiate the false teaching that the church must yet recognize other happenings and powers, images and truths as divine revelation alongside this one Word of God.'

This claim to absolute truth is very different from an expression of anxious uncertainty. Here Christians are opposing a totalitarian 'absolutist' enemy in unconditional resistance, and making a stand against a power which is hostile to humanity and thus to God. In such a situation, dialogue must come to an end and be replaced by an uncompromising claim to exclusiveness. Internally, the hardening of fronts necessitated by external pressure produces a fortress mentality centred on a clear confession.[1] But here, in contrast to an absolutizing of the self as a result of immaturity and weakness, we have the expression of a strong self, and sovereign steadfastness. When conditions change, the same sovereignty can again be expressed in a free and open dialogue. This was also made clear in the late Barth, when he suddenly began to talk of 'lesser lights' outside the Christian faith.[2]

Thus there are manifestly absolute truth-claims which cannot be attributed to personality structures in which the ego is weak; exclusivist claims which do not represent a flight from threatening situations; claims to absoluteness which break up the rigidity of the fundamentalist attitude and are to be understood as a defence of the confession in situations of external danger posed by absolutist totalitarian claims. The Christian fortress mentality can have two faces: it can describe the point of flight of someone with a weak ego; but it can also be adopted by a mature and strong personality which has to protect itself and its faith from acute threat and does so with courage and a readiness for sacrifice.

So we can make a distinction between what I would want to call habitual and situational absolutism. Habitual absolutism is produced by inner structures of the person and therefore is attached to a person as an attitude. It can be recognized by an absolutist reaction to the demands of different situations. By contrast, situational absolutism is a defensive reaction appropriate to a particular situation of threat. It can be recognized by the way in which it casts off the absolutist attitude as soon as the oppressive situation becomes less acute. There is then a possibility of openness towards other truth-claims and dialogue with them.

This distinction is not easy to make in practice, since people with weak egos always appeal to a massive threat from outside as a basis for their absolutist attitude: the dilution of Christian faith in communities which are no longer true to Bible and confession; the general decline in moral values in a consumer-orientated, secularized society; the supposedly imminent advance of militant Islam; the missionary activity of sects and other world religions, etc. It is a characteristic of this type of personality to feel that it and the Christian message are threatened and constantly to have to be on the defensive. Instead of being an exception, the fortress mentality becomes the norm.

The definition of the boundary between real and imagined danger depends strongly on standpoint and perspective: a neutral outside observer will see quite a different picture from that 'seen' from within a fundamentalist circle. But precisely where these perspectives diverge widely, where a small group sees dangers arising for itself and Christian faith which even other Christians do not perceive in the same way, there is no avoiding the question whether the view of reality held is a realistic one. And the answer to this question again depends on whether the 'absolutist' attitude is a deluded over-reaction or a highly reasonable defensive attitude against real threats. The other side of such an extreme overestimation of the real danger is usually an underestimation of the persuasive power of the message of Christ. So it can also be said that such an attitude expresses an anxious lack of faith and trust in God and God's creative Spirit to win through against real dangers – perhaps to win through in a completely different way from what was expected. Now this lack of faith is the precise opposite of what is expressed in the claim to absoluteness which stands as a bulwark in the battle over faith.

My reflections so far have primarily started from the phenomena of modern Christian 'absolutism' which can be observed in the present. What I have described as an 'absolutist attitude' applies to these phenomena and cannot simply be transferred to confessions and forms of doctrine in the history of theology.

Now I want to go back to the beginnings of Christianity and there investigate the theological roots of the claim to absoluteness. Here, too, there are situations of confrontation which have caused this claim to be made. Only such situations of confrontation can explain what, out of context, may seem to our eyes to be religious arrogance.

7

The Roots of the Christian Claim to Absoluteness in the Separation from Judaism

Christianity grew out of Judaism. The detachment of the daughter religion from the mother religion involved deep mutual injuries which formed the beginning of centuries of enmity. The career of the Christian claim to absoluteness began with the Christian claim to complete Judaism.

The more the little Christian community had to recognize that official Judaism (above all the Pharisaic synagogue) was shutting itself off from its message of Jesus Christ as the end and consummation of the law, and was even rejecting it as a heresy and fighting against it, the more vigorous the attacks of those who confessed Christ became. And conversely, the more the latter read the holy scriptures of the Jews in terms of Christ and in so doing found an increasing number of references which – in their view – unmistakably showed him to be the promised Messiah, the sharper became the defence by the Jewish authorities. The mutual separation began.

Old and new disputes within Judaism were brought up and applied to the dispute between Jews and Christians (who originally were no more than one of the Jewish messianic sects). The old ones included the charge of murdering the prophets, which had constantly been raised by Jewish renewal movements against their rulers. Thus Paul also took over this theme and applied it to the crucifixion of Jesus (I Thess.2.15). The new motifs include the dispute as to who was to blame for the destruction of Jerusalem and the temple. In Matt.27.24f. the evangelist shows that the destruction of the temple was God's punishment for the execution of Jesus by the Jews. Here it is interesting to note that the Pharisees also accused the

Jews of being to blame for the destruction of the temple. However, this was not because they did not believe in Jesus; on the contrary, it was because they had too zealously raised expectations of an imminent historical and political deliverance.

The more the confrontation developed on both sides, the wider the separation between Jews and Christians became and thus the more sweeping were the judgments and condemnations. 'The Pharisees and scribes' were simply stylized as the enemies of Christ and the Gospel of John even speaks quite sweepingly of 'the Jews' as the enemies of Jesus. They are said to have persecuted and killed Jesus, the Son of God, and thus committed the greatest possible blasphemy directly against God himself. Here they have shown their true nature: they did not come from God, but the devil was their father (John 8.44). Could God have done other than reject them?

This radically put in question the Jews' claim to election. In the eyes of the Johannine Christians, the Jews had themselves to blame for the withdrawal of their special status before God. The light had come into the darkness but the darkness had not accepted it (John 1.5). And those who did not allow themselves to be illuminated by this light had uttered the verdict of condemnation on themselves.

Thus the first Christians distinguished between 'the Jews' and 'Israel', the people of God. That meant that no longer *all* Jews belonged to the people of God on the basis of their circumcision, but only those who believed in Jesus as the Christ. Membership of the people of God was accordingly no longer decided by biological origin, by 'outward, fleshly circumcision', but by the confession of Christ, the 'inner circumcision of the heart' (Rom.9.6f.; 4.16).

However, this distinction is not a Christian invention; it occurs in a very similar form in contemporary Judaism:[1] the 'spiritual Jews' were distinguished as 'true' Israel from the merely 'natural Jews'; the 'obedient' (practising) Jews from those who were merely 'born Jews' – just as so many present-day Christian groups distinguish between mere 'baptized Christians' and 'real', i.e. active, committed Christians.

Anyone who was born a Jew had the possibility of becoming a 'Jew in the Spirit', but this was not yet automatic. Following John the Baptist, Christians introduced baptism as a mark of the true people of God and thus excluded those who were merely 'born Jews'.

'It was the raising up of faith in Messiah Jesus as a supersessionary covenantal principle – the view that one was not within the true people of God unless one adopted the faith in this form – that caused the break between the Church and Israel.'[2] The distinction between 'fleshly' and 'spiritual' Israel was drawn in order to put the Jews who were unwilling to confess Christ on the level of merely fleshly Israel and to put Christians in the place of the spiritual Israel.[3]

The theory of disinheritance or substitution, according to which God's election and promise had been transferred from the Jews to the church of Christ, which thus now represented the people of God, the new Israel, does not yet appear in Paul.[4] But the author of I Peter already states it (2.9f.), and the theologians of the early church kept developing it.[5] The claim to be the 'true' Israel, the small flock of the truly faithful who would be saved, in contrast to the apostate, stubborn, notoriously unbelieving Jews, laid the foundation on which later Christians could erect their increasingly narrow claims to absoluteness.

> Rather, the crux of the conflict lay in the fact that the Church erected its messianic midrash into a *new principle of salvation*. For christianity, salvation was now found no longer in any observances – ritual or ethical – founded on the torah of Moses, representing the covenant of the past. Rather, salvation was now found solely through faith in the messianic exegesis of the Church about the salvific role of Jesus as Prophet–King–Son of man, predicted by the prophets. Only that community gathered around this cornerstone is God's true people. All others, for whom the covenant of the past was still the foundation for the ongoing people of God, were outside the true covenant.[6]

The relationship of the Christian daughter to the Jewish mother was governed by the claim to have received a more perfect, indeed the final and concluding, form of revelation, whereas the Jews were what A.Cohen has called 'experts for the unfulfilled time'. This claim to superiority in the sense of a claim to finality finds its clearest expression in the Letter to the Hebrews. 'In many and various ways God spoke of old to our fathers by the prophets; but in these last days he has spoken to us by a Son, whom he appointed the heir of all things . . .'(1.1f.). The old covenant is replaced and superseded by the new covenant, which is better than the old (Heb.8.6–13; 7.22).[7] Accordingly, old and new covenants are related as promise to fulfilment, outward form to inner meaning. In Christ, the heavenly high priest, God has brought us redemption once for all (*ephapax*, Heb.9.12), and thus done away with the earthly priesthood of the Levites. The one definitive sacrifice of Christ makes superfluous the whole sacrificial cult of the Levites, who first had to sacrifice for themselves and then, time and again, for the people. This was the foundation of the 'myth of the carnal, legalistic and obsolete Jew'.[8]

For their part, the Jews responded to the increasing polemic of the Christians by breaking off religious fellowship with the Jewish Christians, disparaging Jesus (Acts 18.6) and denouncing Christians to the Roman authorities as troublemakers. Around 100 CE Rabbi Gamaliel added the following petition to the Eighteen Benedictions, which Jews had to say three times a day: 'For the apostates let there be no hope, and let the arrogant government be speedily uprooted in our days. Let the Christians and heretics be destroyed in a moment. And let them be blotted out of the Book of Life . . .'[9]

The mutuality with which the separation between Jews and Christians took place should not be forgotten when we read Adolf von Harnack's apt, though one-sided, verdict on the church's treatment of the Jews: 'Such an injustice as that inflicted by the Gentile church on Judaism is almost unprecedented in the annals of history. The Gentile church stripped it of everything; she took away its holy book; herself but a transformation of Judaism, she cut every connection with the parent religion. The daughter first robbed her mother, and then repudiated her!'[10]

So far we have attempted to see the rise of the Christian claim to superiority above all in connection with the painful separation of Jews and Christians after the destruction of the Jerusalem temple in 70 CE. We have seen that this claim to superiority derived from a sense that God's way with the Jews had reached its goal in Christ. But now we must go a stage further and ask whether Jesus himself had already made this claim to fulfilment or finality (and if so, in what way).

Jesus believed that the expectation of Jewish apocalyptic had come very near, namely the divine revolution in history, the dawn of the end time, i.e. God's judgment and the beginning of a time of salvation for those who withstood the judgment. 'The time is fulfilled, the kingdom of God is at hand. Repent and believe in the gospel' (Mark 1.15). That was his message. Time was pressing; there was an acute need to make a decision. Jesus confronted all his followers with an unconditional either–or. Everything else was secondary compared with the decision over salvation or damnation. Anyone in this situation who put his hand to the plough and looked back was not fit for the kingdom of heaven (Luke 9.62).

'The word which the prophet is conscious of having to speak by God's commission takes the form of the final word, by which God summons men to definitive decision.'[11] That gives it the character of eschatological finality and in that sense absoluteness. Jesus did not so much claim to be superior to the Jewish religious teachers of his time; rather, he claimed to be the last prophet with the final announcement of the coming kingdom of God, the dawn of which was immediately imminent. Whether one would enter this kingdom depended on one's attitude to Jesus' message (Mark 8.38; Luke 9.26; 12.8f.).

When the kingdom of God did not break in as expected, 'as a miraculous world-transforming event',[12] and the one who proclaimed this dawn had to die a shameful death on the cross, his claim to finality seemed finally to have been refuted. But under the impact of their encounter with the risen Christ, a new understanding dawned on the disciples: the claim to finality was still right, and Jesus' death on the cross had not robbed it of its force; however, it had to be related to the crucified Jesus himself: the disciples claimed that the world-shaking event had taken place in his death and resurrection. Certainly this was not as they had expected, but it was in a no less definitive way. Human salvation was decided through faith in him, the one who had been crucified and had risen – in an unconditonal either–or (Mark 8.38; Luke 10.16b). That most Jews rejected this claim was the first step towards the separation described above, which led to bitter enmity towards the Jews in subsequent centuries.[13]

Such antisemitism or anti-Judaism can never be derived from Jesus. He passionately wooed the Jews, and where he entered into judgment on them, he did not do this out of hatred but out of love of his people. And Paul, too, warns Christians against lording it in any way over the Jews. In the image of the olive tree, mentioned above,[14]

Christians are reminded that they have acquired a share in the rich roots of the olive tree (i.e. the people of God) through no merit of their own. This one twig growing from a wild olive tree is not allowed to elevate itself above the branch removed from the noble olive tree because of unbelief. 'If you do boast, remember that it is not you that support the root, but the root that supports you . . . Do not become proud, but stand in awe. For if God did not spare the natural branches, neither will he spare you' (Rom.11.18–21).

One can understand this prohibition against boasting of one's own Christianity (Rom.11.17ff.) as a veto against any claim of Christianity to absoluteness. There is only one legitimate way of boasting: 'Let him who boasts boast in the Lord' (I Cor.1.31; Jer.9.23f.). 'For it is not the man who commends himself that is accepted, but the man whom the Lord commends' (II Cor.10.18). What has been given to the Christians has been given to them through unmerited grace which is not at their disposal. This is a gift that can be lost at any time, on which no one can make a claim. It is wrong to use it as a spiritual instrument for exalting oneself above others.

8

'Claims to Absoluteness' in the Bible

There are some passages in the Bible to which all those who seek biblical justification for their claims to absoluteness always appeal. Let us now look more closely at these passages against the background of the confrontation that was described in the previous chapter. If we put them in the context of the situations from which they arose, it becomes evident how little we have universal judgments on non-Christian religions here. To seek to derive a claim to absoluteness for Christian faith from these passages would be to press them too far. First let us take the Johannine statements about the uniqueness of Jesus Christ.

John 14.6

In John 1.14 + 18; 3.16 + 18 and I John 4.9, Jesus Christ is described as the *only* Son of God. The evangelist wants to bear witness to the exclusiveness of the revelation in Christ. The emphasis on this exclusiveness is a theme of all the discourses of the Johannine Jesus, so that John 1.18 can be described as virtually the 'basic statement of Johannine christology'.[1] Before and outside the only Son there was and is no true knowledge of God (John 1.18; 5.37f.), and after him there is no more revelation nor saving access to God, since in him the last eschatological revelation has taken place: with the sending of the Son the final judgment has broken in (3.17f.; 5.24). This claim is formulated most powerfully in the metaphorical 'I am' sayings of the Gospel of John, for example in John 10.8, where Jesus says, 'I am the door of the sheep. All who came before me are thieves and robbers.' The well-known statement 'I am the way, the truth and the life; no one comes to the Father but through me' (John 14.6) then fits into this context.

53

We can understand this statement only if we think of the oppressed situation of the Johannine community. The Johannine Christians were originally Jews and wanted to remain Jews. With their belief in the messianic redeemer who had been sent as a judge by God they in no way wanted to found their own religion, but to penetrate Judaism. However, in the synagogue this faith met with increasing repudiation. There was a break. The Johannine community was excluded from the synagogue against its will; probably there were violent attacks on it (John 16.2). In bitter enmity and unbridled hatred, accusations were hurled at the Jews of the synagogue: 'He who does not honour the Son does not honour the Father who sent him' (John 5.23). And 'You are of your father the devil, and your will is to do your father's desires. He was a murderer from the beginning and has nothing to do with the truth . . .; when he lies, he speaks according to his own nature, for he is a liar and the father of lies' (John 8.44). The Jews had clearly shown their godlessness in the crucifixion of Jesus: they were murderers of God. The oppressed and persecuted community glorified Christ[2] and condemned all those who did not want to know about this message. 'The denial of the messiahship of Jesus by some may have been matched by its accentuation by others.'[3] The Johannine community reacted to the acute threat from outside by making its own conviction absolute.

The sharp statements which thus arose are to be interpreted as a reaction to a quite specific challenge and not as universally valid suprahistorical judgments on the religions of the world. They cannot simply be transferred to quite different situations; a careful hermeneutical work of translation is needed. Where the background of the situation which led to the polemic no longer exists, the polemic no longer has any justification. But where it is maintained, one must ask in ideological-critical terms in whose interest this is done.

Helmut Gollwitzer provides one example of such a hermeneutical work of translation. He does not want either to adopt the Johannine criticism of the Jews today as a truth which was valid then, nor does he want to 'regret it as a historical aberration and consign it to the archives'.[4] It must be taken seriously, particularly for our day. But taking it seriously does not mean also understanding it today as an attack on the Jews; rather, it should be used as criticism of the church. For just as at that time this criticism was one within Judaism, so now it must be translated into a criticism within Christianity: 'The focus of such words is not on others but, if heard rightly, on ourselves',[5] and here not least on the anti-Judaism among us.

One can agree with the argument put forward by Ulrich Wilckens, the former Bishop of Hamburg and a New Testament scholar, that anti-Judaism is fundamental to the New Testament writings.[6] But one must resolutely oppose him when he concludes from this that such anti-Judaism is also normative for Christianity.[7]

The Johannine Judaism to which evangelicals and Christian fundamentalists constantly refer must also be seen in connection with the sharp dispute between the Johannine sects and the Jewish mother religion.

Already in Deutero-Isaiah (Isa.40–55) there is 'an almost dualistic distinction between two times, the old time of disaster which is now coming to an end and the new time of salvation which is imminent, when salvation will be eternal and immutable (43.18f.; 51.6,8; 54.8,9f.)'.[8] This dualism of the times is transplanted into Jewish apocalyptic with its idea of the two 'aeons' (cosmic powers, world ages). The apocalyptic-dualistic picture of the world then entered the Gospel of John, presumably under the influence of the Qumran community.

The origin of this dualism does not lie in Judaism, but in Persia, in the religion of the prophet Zarathustra (sixth century BCE). In his teaching, the fight between good and evil, between the powers of light and the powers of darkness, plays a decisive role. The prophet promises that it will end with the victory of the good. This sharply exclusive dualism between good and evil, the doctrine of the two world ages (the time of disaster and the time of salvation), and also the notion of the mediators of salvation, angels and the devil, and belief in a heavenly book containing human deeds – all these are revelations of Zarathustra which were taken over by Judaism.[9]

According to Jürgen Becker, the Johannine community went through three theological stages on its way to sectarian isolation: from the Jewish-Christian missionary approach without dualism, through a christologically orientated dualism, to an ecclesiastical dualism.[10] Humankind was divided into two groups: those who 'do the truth' and 'love', and those who 'do evil' and 'hate'; the one group stands in the sphere of light, truth and the spirit, the sphere of God's rule; and the other in darkness, the lie and the flesh, where the devil rules (John 3.19–21).[11] In the one sphere there is eternal life; in the other, death, God's wrath and corruption.

In the so-called 'ecclesiastical redaction' of the Gospel of John the opposition of 'above' and 'below' turned into an opposition of church (community) and world (cosmos). Here we have a very significant root of the church's tendency in later times to make itself absolute: the historical faith community of Christians was given the eschatological qualities of the new creation; it became the imperishable vehicle of the unconcealed truth of God. 'As Jesus is in the Father and the Father is in him, so his disciples abide in Jesus and Jesus in them. Through him, they abide in God, just as he abides in God. They are the extension of his incarnate revelation of God in the world.'[12]

Now where the historical is surrounded with the aura of the ultimately valid, or conversely where the ultimately valid is directly historicized, religious claims to absoluteness arise. And the more strongly a faith community claims this ultimate validity exclusively for itself, and in so doing banishes other forms of believing and other faith communities to the sphere of the merely worldly, if not the demonic, the more easily the spirit of enmity can dominate this religion on its further course through history. Then and only then does what Franz Rosenzweig said about John 14.6 apply: as long as Christianity maintains this statement 'as its authentic dogma, there is no place in it for the living God'.[13]

The Johannine community did not produce this dualism, but it did take it over and develop it. In the isolation into which it was forced, it saw itself as the small elect flock of the Messiah (though its mission had been rejected by the Jews), as the torchbearer of the light. To seek to take this confrontational defensiveness as a model for the attitude of Christians to non-Christians generally would be theologically quite naive, and would have immediate consequences which would quite bluntly have to be called un-Christian.

Jesus was aware of having been sent to the Jews (Matt.15.24), and he also sent his disciples to the Jews (Matt.10.5f.). So he had no occasion to argue with the non-Jewish religions and their gods as such.[14] But in his behaviour he made no distinction in principle between Jews and non-Jews. He even presented non-Jews, pagans, as models of faith, like the Canaanite (Syro-Phoenician) woman whose daughter he healed (Matt.15.21–28), or the (Roman) centurion of Capernaum who asked for help for his sick servant (Matt.8.5–13). When Jesus sat by the Samaritan woman at the well and even spent two days in her village (John 4), he was breaking a tabu: it was forbidden to Jews to have contact with the despised Samaritans. Furthermore, in the parable of the good Samaritan he presented the Jews with a man from Samaria whom they regarded as godless in the function of an unselfish helper (Luke 10.29–37). Jesus was indifferent to religious and social barriers where the salvation of men and women was at stake. Perhaps he even had no occasion to engage in argument with non-Jewish religions and their gods because he knew that pagans,[15] like Jews, were ultimately included in God's all-embracing will for salvation.

Acts 4.12

Acts 4.12, 'Luke's way of asserting that Christianity is absolute',[16] arose out of a situation in which there was an acute danger for individual Christians: 'And there is salvation in no one else, for there is no other name under heaven given among men by which we must be saved.'[17]

This statement was made by Peter, 'filled with the Holy Spirit', to his accusers. The leader of the Jews had brought him in for interrogation and required him to explain by what power and in what name he had healed a man born lame at the Beautiful Gate in Jerusalem. Thereupon Peter confessed that this healing had taken place in the name of Jesus. In 4.12b this individual ('therapeutic') act of healing is then transferred to 'our' ('spiritual') salvation. The healing of a lame man becomes the proclamation of the universal, eschatological significance of Jesus for salvation.

Whether the trial scene described here really took place in this form is highly questionable – most exegetes are agreed on that. But the beginning of the persecution of the first Christians by the Jewish leaders (Pharisees, Sadducaean priests and lay nobility) is clearly expressed in it (cf. Luke 11.49). The attacks come to a climax with the execution of Stephen (Acts 7) and James (Acts 12). After the Jewish War (66–70 CE), the earliest Jewish community had to flee from Jerusalem. Acts was written not long afterwards (between 80 and 90 CE).

If the background to John 14.6 was the threat to a whole community, in Acts 4.12 there is the threat of the condemnation and death of the leader of the community. So in both cases we have real confessional situations, situations in which people safeguard their own power of resistance by retreating into the foundations of their faith and hurling their beliefs at their attackers with the courage of confessors.

Colossians 1.15–20

The hymn to the Colossians (1.15–20) shows that there were also quite different situations of danger in which biblical writers glorified Jesus Christ with 'absolute' predicates. Karl-Josef Kuschel interprets the hymn in terms of the situation of the author and the community to whom he is writing.[18] 'Anyone who isolates this text from its epistolary and socio-cultural context may discover here a powerful document of Christian superiority, written only fifty years after Jesus' death. For as a Christian can one go further than to claim that one's Christ was already the mediator of God at creation and that all things "in heaven and on earth" were not only created by him and for him but also have their existence in him? . . . If one projects this text or other scriptural texts directly on the present-day dialogue with non-Christian religions, the consequences are quickly drawn: if "everything" is created through Christ and for him, then the religions of the world, too, are parts of this reality of God in creation. At the same time it follows from this that any non-Christian religion is to be relativized in terms of the rule of Christ in the world, indeed in some circumstances to be understood as "heresy" or even as an "eschatological anti-Christian power of seduction". Their position is one of complete dependence on him who "in all things has the pre-eminence"' [392].

However, a completely different picture emerges if one takes into account the contemporary context in which the hymn came into being. First of all there is the author, who identifies himself with Paul: he is a political prisoner. With concern he follows the developments in the community of Colossae, but his hands are tied, and he cannot intervene. First – we may assume – there is still anxiety there about the cosmic forces and elemental powers, since the area around Colossae had been badly damaged by an earthquake in 61 CE. And secondly, dubious philosophical teachings and religious practices are spreading through the community.

'So if we read the hymn in this context, in the context of existential anxiety, the experience of imprisonment, conflict and concern over rivalry, the statements about Christ hardly derive from triumphalist feelings, desires for exclusiveness or the need to be superior. On the contrary, what we have in Col.1.15-20 is simply a hymn of trust and hope by someone who in this corner of the Roman empire, endangered by earthquakes, attempts despite everything to defend his Christian faith, literally in fetters . . .' [394].

He glorifies Christ and praises him as the image of God, to whom all thrones and rules, powers and authorities, are subject. He writes against the anxiety and confusion in Colossae, and against all appearances seeks to proclaim: Jesus Christ is the Lord, trust in him, then anxiety cannot get the better of you.

As Kuschel sums it up: 'An absoluteness (in the sense of being detached from everything), an exclusiveness (in the sense of an unhistorical isolation) and superiority (in the sense of an arrogant superiority) of Jesus Christ is thus not asserted in this letter itself; indeed, that would be to betray the spirit of this hymn, which explicitly speaks of the reconciliation and peace brought by Christ (1.20). Not arrogance, but gratitude and humility, would be the appropriate basic attitude of someone seized by the spirit of this hymn. Any claim to absoluteness and superiority divides and causes dissension. It is part of the signature of the "old man"' [396].

Claims to absoluteness – credal prayers

The biblical passages constantly cited to support the Christian claim to absoluteness are to be understood against their specific backgrounds. Only when they are detached from these backgrounds and given the status of universally valid eternal truths which can be applied to Islam as much as to liberal Christianity do they really become claims to absoluteness. But in such 'dehistoricization' which turns them into timeless dogmas without a context they are misunderstood.

Put in the contexts in which they were composed, the texts read quite differently from the understanding of them as verdicts on non-Christian religions which at this time either did not exist (like Islam) or played no role in the religious and cultural landscape of

Palestine (like the Far Eastern religions). They are not decrees of eternal truths of God without a situation, revealed by Christ about himself, but confessions of him by his disciples and followers. They are not to be understood as metaphysical assertions about divine facts but as an existential expression of unconditional commitment and obligation, as an expression of trust and hope in situations which are desperate.

What stand out here as totalitarian claims to absoluteness are 'statements in the witness box',[19] personal or communal testimony. Such statements first of all express the depth and seriousness of the person's own relationship to God in the face of external threats. The power of God is adduced against the powers from which the danger stems. One might might almost say that this power is conjured up. So the Bible's supposed claims to absoluteness are simply public prayers of confession addressed to the oppressors and the oppressed alike and ultimately to God himself. In theological terms, they have the character of a confession and a doxology. Anyone who tears them from their historical foundation, generalizes them and uses them to condemn non-Christian religions is thus falsifying their original character.

Such confessional prayers express anyhting but self-glorification. They are uttered by those who are imprisoned and persecuted, by potential martyrs, not by emperors and the triumphant.

But they were very soon to be taken over by emperors and the triumphant. When Christianity had won through against the other cults and had been elevated to a state religion, it gained the legal and political, and then also the military, means of turning its religious claims to truth into the church's claim to domination and indeed of imposing it. The bastion erected as protection against threats became a fortress from which Christians threatened, dominated and oppressed those of other faiths. The fortress which was a defence against attackers turned into an offensive post against those of other faiths. The glorification of God in situations of despair became an instrument of repression.

But before we turn to this manifestation of the Christian claim to absoluteness, which has achieved sorry notoriety in church history, we must first concern ourselves with another defensive war in early Christianity.

9

The Roots of the Christian Claim to Absoluteness in the Fight against Hellenistic Syncretism

The painful detachment of Christianity from its mother religion left behind in Christianity an anti-Jewish 'mother complex' from which at all times in church history it was possible to construct a picture of the enemy. The decisive step in this detachment was the resolve to carry the message of Christ beyond Judaism into the non-Jewish, i.e. 'pagan' world. Thereafter Christianity spread rapidly in the Hellenistic world of the Roman empire. But there it did not enter a sphere which was free of religion, but a multi-religious culture in which the individual ways and doctrines of salvation interpenetrated and mixed with one another.

First of all there were the mystery religions: the cults of Eleusis and Dionysus from Greece, the cults of Cybele (Magna Mater) and Attis from Asia Minor, the cults of Isis and Osiris (Serapis) from Egypt, Adonis from Syria, and Mithras from Persia, which was particularly widespread in Rome. They, too, promised their adherents salvation through liberation from the rule of the world and death, by participation in the dying and rising of the deity. The cults were not exclusive; one could be initiated into several of them. In addition (above all in Mesopotamia and Syria), there were the astral religions in which heavenly and astral deities were worshipped as cosmic world powers (for example, the Syrian Baals). From Persia the strictly dualistic religion of Zarathustra exerted an influence. Moreover, not a few contemporaries found a substitute religion in philosophy, in the Stoa, in Platonism, in the teaching of Epicurus or in the religious philosophy of Gnosticism.[1]

Magic, manticism, astrology and the use of oracles were also part of the religion of the time, as was belief in miracle workers like Apollonius of Tyana, to whom people attributed the power to drive out demons and raise the dead.

By contrast, the Roman imperial cult did not play a significant role in the early period of Christianity. It goes back to the divinization of rulers in Egypt, Babylon and Persia. It was first developed when the writing was on the wall for the empire and the collapse of an imperial consciousness began, i.e. first in the time of Decius (249–251), Aurelian (270–275) and Diocletian (284–305). Now it was no longer necessary just for the state gods (like Mithras) to be worshipped; the image of the emperor or the emperor himself was to be worshipped as a manifestation of God, and this was intolerable for Christians.

Syncretism flourished in this multi-religious world, and religions fused: oriental gods were identified with Greek gods (the so-called *interpretatio Graeca* or *interpretatio Romana*), and the figures of Greek gods and their stories conversely took on oriental features. For example, Hermes, the Greek messenger of the gods and god of merchants, was identified with the Egyptian Thoth, and as Hermes Trismegistos was given the office of the all-wise Logos redeemer. Such 'theocrasia' took place above all in the cult of the 'Panthea', Isis.[2]

A thoroughly monotheistic tendency underlay these fusions. The multiplicity of gods was to be understood as a multiplicity of manifestations (or names) of the one God. Just as the sun or the moon or the sea are the same for all people, but could be given different names, so too the individual gods were seen as superficial revelations of the one great divine mystery which cannot be known 'in itself'.[3] So this is a monotheism which does not do away with polytheism, but functionalizes the individual gods and subordinates them to the supreme God (e.g. Helios Apollo) or identifies them with him. Thus attempts were also made to incorporate the God of the Jews and Christians into this system, say by identifying him with Dionysus[4] or seeing him represented by Zeus.[5] The different saviours were also said ultimately to represent one and the same figure, a figure which simply had different names among the different peoples: thus Christ could be identified in Gnostic sects with Hermes, Horus, Mithras, etc. This notion – in which neo-

Platonic thought was reflected – led to the conviction that the different religions were different ways to the same God. Thus it was possible to combine Christian rites with 'pagan' ones. The rulers encouraged this development, hoping to gain from it the demolition of potential for inter-religious conflict – in the interest of stabilizing the political order and their rule.[6]

Christianity found itself in an environment which allowed it to exist as one religion among many, and to spread. The limits of state tolerance were reached only where there was doubt as to the political loyalty of Christians (and Jews) or where people were looking for a scapegoat. In such cases there could be persecutions, but these always remained regional.

Much as Christians made use of the relative freedom of religion, they resisted being given the status of one religious community among many. They were afraid that competition on the open religious market with its attractive offers would drain the Christian religion of its best as a contribution to the great mix. They reacted to this spiritual threat, which was 'mild' in that it was not physical, in two ways. Anything that contradicted basic Christian convictions was excluded. But Christians took over from the religions and philosophy anything that could be of use in explaining and understanding the message of Christ, 'baptizing' it, i.e. subjecting it to a Christian reinterpretation. So when Paul speaks, say, in Rom.6 of dying with Christ, he is taking up a theme from the mystery religions,[7] in order to relate it to the participation of the Christian in the dying and rising of Christ.

Christians also fought vehemently against any fusion of their God or saviour. As they took up the dominant tendency towards monotheism, so they uncompromisingly did away with subordinate deities.[8]

However, the battle of young Christianity to safeguard its identity in a syncretistic environment deeply changed Christianity itself. Adolf von Harnack spoke of the battle against syncretistic 'Gnosticism' and described the change which this controversy brought with it as the 'acute Hellenization of Christianity'. 'But struggle in this case meant definition, that is to say, drawing a sharp line of demarcation around what was Christian and declaring everything heathen that would not keep within it. *The struggle with Gnosticism compelled the Church to put its teaching, its worship, and its discipline into fixed forms and ordinances, and to exclude everyone who would not yield them obedience.* In the conviction that it was everywhere merely conserving and honouring what had been handed down, it never for a moment doubted that the obedience which it demanded was anything more than subjection to the divine will itself, and that in the doctrines with which it encountered the enemy it was exhibiting the impress of religion itself.'[9] The price that Christianity had to pay for warding off Hellenistic syncretism was a high one. For the church, 'by becoming a community with a fully worked out scheme of doctrine, and a definite form of public worship . . . was of necessity compelled to take on forms analogous to those which it combated in the Gnostics . . . It was now forced to say, "You are no Christian, you cannot come into any relation at all with God, unless you have first of all acknowledged these doctrines, yielded obedience to these ordinances and followed out definite forms of mediation". Thus 'what was set up as a protection against enemies from without became the palladium, indeed the very foundation within.'[10] The foundations were developed and increasingly fortified even when the threat had passed.

Warding off Hellenistic syncretism turned the church into a hierarchical institution, led by priests, bishops and the pope. It developed its faith on the model of Greek thought into a universal philosophy of God and the world, and thus took over on a broad front the Platonic dualism of the material and the ideal, the temporal and the eternal, the mortal and the immortal, the bodily (fleshly) and the spiritual, the changeable and the unchangeable, the finite and the infinite.[11] The Greek understanding of the truth with its strict either-or logic[12] came to govern theology, which was thus 'logified' into theo-*logy*. The 'principle of contradiction' which was fundamental to this understanding of the truth ran: if two statements are contradictory, only one of them can be true and the other must be false. More precisely, something that is, cannot not be, at the same time and in the same respect. Therefore alongside the one truth there can only be untruth, falsehood, lies and error. And this dualism of 'true and false' became a quite distinctive root for the Christian claim to absoluteness.

In addition, Roman legal thought proved influential. Under its influence faith was codified, i.e. moulded in the fixed form of a quasi-legal rule of church codes and theological doctrines.

The Greek logification and the Roman codification consolidated belief in Christ into an intellectualistic and legalistic orthodoxy which laid down what was necessary for faith and thus for salvation. But in so doing, it also drew the boundaries between belief and unbelief, and excluded all those seeking God by other ways.

It may be necessary to draw boundaries in order to safeguard the centre. But where the boundaries become a *definition* of the centre, that Christian fanaticism can arise which not only cuts back the spirit of freedom to the criterion of right doctrine but also boasts that it has the competence to persecute those with other beliefs.

The trauma of syncretism arose in the struggle of early Christianity against the multi-religious culture of the Hellenistic world. It still has an influence today, and provokes vigorous defensive reactions among Christians. Many see clear parallels between then and now. 'Is not our present situation comparable to that of Hellenistic syncretism?', they ask. We too live in a society which is becoming increasingly multi-religious, which allows an individual freedom of religion and thus classifies Christianity as one religious community among many (albeit with special privileges). All may be active in this pluralistic field as long as they observe particular social rules of the game. And that includes accepting pluralism. Religion is a private affair, and cannot claim any universal social monopoly. And there are already even Christian theologians who teach that all religions are to be seen as equally legitimate ways to salvation.[13]

That provokes critics who see this kind of openness to dialogue as an impossible renunciation of theological truth; their argument is that if the church had not opposed the undertow of syncretism, it would have died from a diffusion of its identity. And because the same danger exists today, it must demarcate its message today with the same decisiveness as it did then and protect it from being dissolved into general religiosity. Not only are other religions to be fought against, but first and foremost the liberal attitude of assimilation among Christians themselves.[14]

One of the best-known recent examples of such criticism was polemic against the address given by the Korean theologian Chung Hyun Kyung at the beginning of the Seventh General Assembly of the World Council of Churches in Canberra.[15] Here too it was again the charge of syncretism which was brought against her attempt to express the working of the Holy Spirit in terms and rites drawn from the Confucian, Shamanic and Buddhist traditions of Korea.[16]

Some critics even go so far as to see the present situation of Christian faith and the Christian communities in Western Europe generally as a permanent confessional battle against pluralism and syncretism and carry on bitter fights for the true faith: 'Unless all signs are deceiving, today we are engaged in a struggle for the faith, a church struggle, compared to which the church struggle of the Third Reich was a preliminary skirmish. The uncanny thing is that today's struggle is often barely recognized, is usually trivialized, and goes under the guise of "pluralism".' Thus the former bishop Dr Hermann Dietzfelbinger.[17]

Those who see the struggle of the Confessing Church against the Fascist Nazi regime as a mere skirmish preliminary to a gigantic confessional struggle allegedly taking place at present in Western Christianity must seriously ask themselves whether their perception accords with reality. And those who set themselves above the defenders of the Christian confession against the Nazi ideology in the church struggle during the Third Reich who lost their lives in the process (like Dietrich Bonhoeffer, Paul Schneider and Adolf Delp) must ask themselves whether they are not dishonouring these martyrs.

Calls to preserve pure Christianity from the undertow of the areligious or multireligious environment overlook the fact that such preservation can never succeed. For there can never be a pure form of Christianity, nor has there ever been one – Christianity has always been adapted to its cultural context ('inculturated'), though without being assimilated into it. It was never alive, creative and thus attractive where it barricaded itself in and vaunted itself in increasingly narrow claims to validity, but only where it was open to controversy and competition with its cultural and religious environment. It won through, not where it claimed validity but where it proved to be the better way. Its strength was decided not by its truth-claim but by the way in which it proved itself.

Secondly, such calls overlook the fact that the historical success of Christianity in the Roman empire, its victory over the other religions, was not due merely to the effort to preserve pure Christianity. Precisely because the Christian religion could incorporate and surpass everything that was valuable to non-Christians about their religions, it was in a position to suppress these religions. It was not least the capacity of Christianity to integrate, or, to put it pointedly, its capacity for syncretism, which played a by no means small part in its success.[18]

Thirdly, these calls overlook the fact that in reality attempts to preserve pure Christianity only lead to a hardening of forms of Christian faith and life. The fixing of such forms does not mean that they are elevated above all times; on the contrary, it means that they are conditioned by a particular time and a particular culture. Such a fixing cuts off from each time the power of the Christian message which is to be expressed anew and, where it is coupled with power, leads to a repressive intolerance that contradicts the heart of the Christian message. For this message does not preach the domination of a doctrine and its representatives, but proclaims the rule of God who in unbounded love seeks to bring about reconciliation among people.

That is not to say that the repudiation of Hellenistic 'Gnosticism' did not really take place, or that it was an error; beyond question it was necessary for the survival of the Christian faith. Similarly, the fight against the totalitarian ideology of the Nazis was necessary beyond any doubt, just as in the present it is necessary to fight sharply against some forms of the so-called new religions – like the cult of Satan and popular neopaganism.[19]

But this fight against the excrescences of neo-religious sectarianism is to be distinguished completely from the encounter with the great world religions and their rich traditions. Just as in the syncretism of late antiquity Christians fought against magic, hermetics and theurgy, so today they may attack pseudo-religious occult practices which destroy personality, but not religions in which millions of people have lived meaningful lives for many centuries.

As for the struggle of the early church against Hellenism, Greek philosophy and Judaism, we must ask critically whether this struggle was proportionate to the issue. Are all means appropriate in the fight for the message of God's saving presence in Jesus Christ? May one put love of neighbour in the background and condemn opponents as though one were sitting on God's judgment seat? Has not the proclamation of the love of God to submit to the logic of love, which forbids it any use of violence?[20]

Secondly, we must ask whether a confrontation must not be abandoned once the threat is past. In the early church this happened only to a very limited degree: the militant attitude hardened into the expression of a real zeal for faith.[21] The less energy the battle against the outside threat required, the more energy was turned inwards, in the dispute of various church parties over the only true faith. The vigour of this struggle can be explained not least from the fact that theological positions had been combined with political positions, in the church and also in the state.

'Men put an end to brotherly fellowship for the sake of a nuance, and thousands were cast out, condemned, loaded with chains and done to death. It is a gruesome history. On the question of "christology" men bent their religious doctrines into terrible weapons, and spread fear and intimidation everywhere. This attitude still continues; christology is treated as though the gospel had no other problem to offer, and the accompanying fanaticism is still rampant in our own day.'[22]

From the Claim to Absoluteness to State Control

The Christian faith spread rapidly throughout the Roman empire and gained increasing significance. With the so-called Edict of Milan (313 CE), Constantine the Great brought about a change in Christianity which was to transform it from being a persecuted religion into a recognized religion and then the sole state religion. In 341 CE superstition and sacrifice carried the death penalty, and in 346 the non-Christian temples were closed. 'Now began an attack on the temples which unleashed the wildest fanaticism of the Christian mob.'[1]

Whereas the Christians had previously been more or less persecuted, now in their turn they persecuted the adherents of the pagan cults in the Roman empire. Around 347 the Sicilian orator J.Firmicus Maternus in his diatribe *On the Error of Pagan Religions* called on the emperors Constantius II and Constans to exterminate pagan religion: 'These (pagan) practices must be eradicated, exterminated and removed ... so that the crude error of this madness no longer stains the Roman world . . .It is better for you to free them (the pagans) against their will than to allow them willingly to fall to destruction.'[2]

On 28 February 380 Theodosius the Great then enacted the edict *Cunctos populos*, which stated: 'It is our will that all people over whom we exercise a mild and moderate government should persevere in the religion which the divine apostle Peter . . . has handed down to the Romans . . . namely, that according to the instruction of the apostles and the teaching of the gospel we believe in one Godhead of Father, Son and Holy Spirit in equal majesty and holy Trinity. We command that only those who follow this law may be called Catholic

Christians; the rest whom we regard as foolish and senseless have to bear the infamy of heretical teaching. Nor may their places of assembly be called churches. In the end they face divine retribution, but they are also hastening towards our penal justice which has been committed to us by the judgment of heaven.'[3]

The prohibition of all non-Christian cults in 391 made the Christian church the state church, and paganism and heresy a state crime. Since they had been banned, all non-Christian cults were legally regarded as *religiones falsae*, false religions. By comparison, Christianity presented itself as the true religion, *religio vera*. The Theodosian Code collects laws of Roman emperors against the adherents of false religions. These turned into state law the theory that Christian theologians had been forming in previous centuries: first of all defensively in the face of pagan attacks, and then increasingly on the offensive in a counter-attack on the world of non-Christian religion and philosophy.[4] The three most important apologists of Christianity as *vera religio* are the three North Africans Tertullian, Cyprian and Lactantius.

The hot-blooded Tertullian (c.150–200) had a nature which 'fights rather than loves, breaks rather than bends, and which has accepted with joy the "service", the *militia Christi*. He loves to conjure up military metaphors, because it is not a matter of agreement but of decision.'[5] The 'philosophizing advocate', as Adolf von Harnack called him, introduced the acuteness of Roman legal thought into Latin Christianity. He deliberately chose the form of the law court speech for his *Apology*, in which he addresses 'the heads of the Roman government'[6] – but indirectly all paganism. Here he presents the doctrine and life of Christians in order to refute the accusations brought against them. He states unequivocally that Christianity is the only true religion (the *vera religio veri Dei*[7]) because it rests on God's revelation. Here – and here alone – God has made himself, his nature and his will known. Anything that deviates from this truth ultimately amounts to seduction by demons, God's enemies. So paganism 'is to Tertullian no foolishness to be enlightened, no prejudice or mistake which can be dispelled or brought to reason. It is "the world", and as such a great demonic unity to be recognized in its entirety, and to be rejected and condemned'.[8] In essence, according to Tertullian, pagan hostility to

God consists in a blurring of the boundaries between God and creation: its nature is to idolize the creature, and polytheism goes with it.

Even sharper than Tertullian's polemic against paganism is his attack on the Gnostic heresies which were spreading in Christianity. Here he did not need to exercise any tactical caution in view of the power of the authorities. For here it was no longer a question of justifying Christianity in the face of the pagan authorities; here the battle for the true faith had to be fought out within Christianity. So his prime concern was not 'to understand his opponents from the point of view of their own presuppositions or to do justice to their "concern" of the moment. He seeks to expose them and time and again pours forth against them his biting sarcasm'.[9] In his *Prescriptions against the Heretics*, Tertullian defends the church's legal claim to the possession of the truth. For it received this truth directly from Christ through the apostles – long before the heretical false teaching came into being. 'This is my property; I have long possessed it; I possessed it before you; I hold sure title deeds from the original owners themselves to whom the property belonged. I am the heir of the apostles; but you have surely forfeited it for ever and are utterly cast out, as strangers, as enemies.'[10]

Tertullian's claim to exclusive possession of the truth can also be explained from his radical rejection of philosophy, which for him is no more than vain fantasizing, the wisdom of the world, foolishness before God. Why engage in philosophical speculations? Why construct 'a Stoic and Platonic and dialectical Christianity'?[11] All truth is contained in Christ and his gospel: one must believe in that alone. A quest for the truth makes sense only where the truth is not known; where it is known, the quest must have an end. 'What has Athens to do with Jerusalem, what has the academy to do with the church, what have heretics to do with Christians?'[12] Nothing!

Tertullian gave the church ample grounds for understanding itself as the sole guardian of God's truth. His pupil Cyprian of Carthage (c.205–258), a man of a much more moderate, quiet and aristocratic nature than Tertullian, though no less a hard-liner than he was, developed them into a new understanding of the church which immediately became normative. For Cyprian, the church was no longer primarily the spiritual communion of saints (i.e. those who truly believe and thus are saved) but an institution with a hierarchical organization under the leadership of the bishop. Membership of it, the bride of Christ, is the indispensable presupposition for attaining salvation. 'She knows one home; she guards with chaste modesty the sanctity of one church. She keeps us for God. She appoints the sons whom she has borne for the kingdom. Whoever is separated from the church and is joined with an adulteress [i.e. a schismatic "church"] is separated from the promises of the church; nor can he who forsakes the church of Christ attain to the rewards of Christ. He is a stranger; he is profane; he is an enemy. He can no longer have God for his father, who does not have the church for his mother.'[13] And in one of his letters, almost in passing, a statement appears which was to have a far-reaching effect: *salus extra ecclesiam non est* – there is no salvation outside the church.[14] The church is one, even if there are many variations within this unity: 'God is one and Christ is one, and his church is one and the faith is one and the people ... Whatever has proceeded from the womb cannot live and breathe in its detached condition, but loses the substance of health.'[15]

The writing *On the Unity of the Catholic Church* from which these quotations come 'grew wholly out of the situation of the time'.[16] Under the pressure of the persecution of Christians under Decius in 249 CE, many members of the church of Carthage had denied their faith and left the community. When many of them later wanted to be received back, there was a deep division in the communities. Some of those who had resisted persecution believed that they had been endowed with the Spirit of God in a special way and now claimed the right to forgive the apostates their sins. By contrast, Cyprian insisted that only he as bishop had this right. So he was fighting for the unity of his church under his leadership. That there is no salvation outside the church is not said to non-Christians but to apostate members of the community. And the call to restore the unity of the church under the leadership of the bishop is addressed to those who claim the right to forgive sins.

Nor was this statement meant as the decree of a universally valid truth about access to – and exclusion from – salvation. But it was very soon detached from its setting and generalized. So it became the classic formulation of the Christian claim to absoluteness, which had binding authority in the Catholic church down to the Second Vatican Council.[17]

The monumental *magnum opus* of Lactantius (c.250–340), the seven books of the *Divine Institutions*, is very much dominated by the distinction between *vera et falsa religio*. Pagan belief in gods is rejected as falsehood and of no account. Christ, the Son of God, first taught the true knowledge of God and secondly, through his sacrificial death, performed the decisive work of redemption. Both truth and grace have been preserved in the Catholic church: '. . . thus there remains for men only one hope, and this lies in adhering to the true religion and the true wisdom which is Christ; anyone who does not know Christ remains for ever separated by a gulf from the truth and from God'.[18] There is only one way of life and one way of death; one leads to heaven and the other to hell. By his incarnation in Jesus Christ God has shown 'us' the way of life.[19]

When Constantine came to power, the theological distinction between true and false religion was sanctioned by state law. In a letter to the priest Celsus he already shows the sense of mission on the part of the Christian ruler who regards it as his task to see to the proclamation of the true religion and to remove all error.[20] So the church could call on him and hold him to this task when movements developed within or without which it saw as a danger. This happened over the new religion of Manichaeanism – a mixture of ancient Persian dualism and Christian Gnosticism with a strictly ascetic life-style, deriving from the Persian Mani (215–273) – which presented itself as a higher, spiritualized form of Christianity. Manichaeism was the first and only 'post-Christian' religion before the spread of Islam.

Religions and philosophies which had arisen *before* Christ's appearance could – if so desired – be judged with relative mildness.[21] It was not their fault that they did not know *the* truth. Nor did they offend against the Christian claim to finality. But a religion which was arrogant enough to claim to go beyond the one and only truth of God in Christ once this had been made known, as Mani did, inevitably seemed a demonic seduction and thus had to be fought against. So this religion was banned in the Roman empire from the beginning. From 382, membership of it bore the death penalty, and its adherents had to meet in secret groups.

73

For a while Augustine (354–430) himself succumbed to the fascination of this rigorist religion, but in his work *On True Religion* (391) he had a reckoning with it. So again it was from a confrontation that church ('catholic') Christianity asserted itself as the true religion. Augustine sees Manichaeism as 'a danger to his religion, posed by the fact that the bearers of another [the Manichaean] religion show a greater enthusiasm and an apparently more intense and powerful faith.'[22]

'This being so,' Augustine writes, 'religion is to be sought neither in the confusion of the pagans, nor in the offscourings of the heretics, nor in the insipidity of the schismatics, nor in the blindness of the Jews, but only among those who are called catholic or orthodox Christians, that is, guardians of truth and followers of right . . .'[23] The nature of false religion lies in the way in which it clings to the world, the body and the senses. In the ascent to purely spiritual truth the Christian has to overcome all wordliness, bodiliness and sensuality – the source of all sin and all error.

This idealism which shuns the world is combined with a sharp dualism, both features which Augustine took over above all from the 'false religion' of Manichaeism.[24] Two kingdoms, two cosmic powers, are locked in combat: the divine kingdom of grace (*civitas Dei*) and the kingdom of the world, the flesh, self-love (*civitas terrena*). The one comes from God and is moving towards eternal bliss (so Augustine can also call it *civitas coelestis*); the other is of the devil and leads to the eternal torments of hell (hence also the designation *civitas Diaboli*). Who belongs to the one city and who belongs to the other, who is saved and who is damned, is laid down from eternity. God has predestined this because he knows human works in advance.

Augustine does not simply identify the earthly church with the *civitas dei*.[25] It is moving towards the city of God, but as long as it has not yet reached this goal, there are not only true but also false Christians in it. In the time after Augustine, however, this identification was often made – with reference to Augustine's doctrine of the two kingdoms – and thus absoluteness was claimed for Christianity, i.e. for the Catholic church.

The pagan religions increasingly disappeared from Christian view, so there was no longer any reason to distinguish between the

74

vera religio and the *falsae religiones*. Religion was the church and the church religion. Other cults – where there still were any – were no longer called 'religion'. The question of *vera religio* reappears only with Nicolas of Cusa (1401–1464).[26]

In a situation in which outward pressure declined, the sharp claims to validity put forward by Christianity were not reduced, but were thought to have been successful and were further consolidated. This happened, for example, by backing up theological confessions with legal prohibitions, as in the closing statement of the Chalcedonian Definition of 451.[27] This is even clearer in the Athanasian Creed (first half of the seventh century), which begins with the assertion: 'Whosoever will be saved: before all things it is necessary that he hold the Catholic Faith. Which faith except everyone do keep whole and undefiled: without doubt he shall perish everlastingly.'[28]

It was the Augustinian contrast between the Christian and the anti-Christian which led 'to the notion of a divinely-willed battle between the Christian realm and the non-Christian world powers, i.e. the intellectual basis of the idea of the Crusades'.[29]

The Claim to Absoluteness –
The Foundation for the Theology
of the Crusades

Christianity's claim to absoluteness as being the only true religion laid the spiritual foundation for the victory of the church over the pagan cults and its recognition by the state. In this process the claim itself changed, in that the claim to truth was combined with a claim to rule – and specifically this meant with a claim on the rulers. What was originally a reference to faith and its object – the message of Christ – now became a designation of the church, which understood itself as the sole guardian and mediator of this message. Now the church was represented by the bishops, with the Bishop of Rome at their head. The popes with increasing vigour applied the claim to absoluteness to the papacy.

Thus massive power interests came into play which needed theological legitimation. And this legitimation was provided by the claim to be able to offer the only way to salvation (and also the need to safeguard this). With this 'imperialism' of salvation the claim to absoluteness became an instrument which justified the church's structures of rule (with a concern for self-preservation and consolidation). It became an instrument of domination. Conversely, there was an unconditional requirement for the church to defend this claim itself where danger threatened.

Since the conquest of Manichaeism, at least dangers from outside – from the sphere of the non-Christian religions – seemed finally to have been banished. The establishment of the Christian religion everywhere could be taken as confirmation of its character as *vera religio*, which it had proved to be historically. But then an event took place which shattered this certainty in a traumatic way, an event which posed the utmost danger to the church and dramatically radicalized its attitude to the religions. Islam appeared on the scene of world history. And in only 100 years an Arab-Islamic world empire had spread rapidly beyond Arabia – to the Near East and Persia, Egypt and North Africa, south-east Europe and Spain – in the process conquering many ancestral Christian lands, above all those of Byzantine Christianity. This explosive expansion caused fear and trembling among Christians. And it put in question their previous view of the history of religion and thus their self-understanding. How could God allow a *post*-Christian religion which claimed to surpass and complete Christianity to win such a victory? A religion which claimed to have received the final revelation of God and therefore to be the true religion, and which was thus lauching a frontal attack on the revelation of Christ?

Manichaeism had always been regarded as a Christian heresy, and the recognition in fact implied that it contained a certain degree of truth (albeit corrupted). An attempt was made to apply this interpretation to Islam as well. But the more the recognition gained ground that the Muslims were not Christians and did not even want to be, but rather stubbornly disputed that Jesus Christ was the only Son of God, the clearer it became that here more than just a Christian heresy had arisen from the abyss. Thus people began to apply the apocalyptic visions of the biblical Revelation of John to Islam and developed a view which entered the collective sub-consciousness of Western Christianity and deeply shaped its attitude to Islam. This was the view of Islam as the 'final power of temptation'[1] announced by God: Muhammad is the false prophet of Rev.19.20. With him Antichrist (or at least his forerunner) has appeared, who can be recognized (according to I John 2.22) by his denial of the Son of God. The beast from the abyss prophesied in Rev.11.7; 17.8 is here, or is very near,[2] 'therefore we know that it is the last hour' (I John 2.18). This explanation appears for the first time in developed form in John of Damascus, the last great church father of the East.[3]

Under Caliph Omar this 'power of temptation' had already conquered Jerusalem in 638. In the following centuries Christians, Muslims and Jews lived there in relative harmony. However, from the tenth century the ruling Fatimid Caliphs of Egypt began to harass the Christians living in Jerusalem and those making pilgrimage there. This pressure further intensified when the Turkish Seldjuks defeated the Fatimids in 1070 and took possession of the Holy Land. The homecoming pilgrims reported this oppression and often exaggerated it. Pope Gregory VII used these reports as the occasion for his resolve to come to the help of the Eastern Christians at the head of a host of knights. In 1095 Pope Urban II then called for the First Crusade with these words: 'A godless people has the cradle of our salvation, the fatherland of the Lord, the motherland of religion, in its power. The godless people of the Saracens has long been oppressing with its tyranny the holy places which were trodden by the feet of the Lord and is holding the faithful in servitude and subjection. "The dogs have entered the sanctuary and the Holy of Holies has been desecrated." The people who worship the true God have been humiliated; the chosen people are having to suffer unworthy oppression. Dear brothers, arm yourselves with the zeal of God, gird your swords to your sides, equip yourselves and be sons of the Mighty One! It is better to die in battle than to see our people and the saints suffering. Let anyone who is zealous for the law of God join us. We want to help our brothers. Go forth, and the Lord will be with you. Turn your weapons ... against the enemies of the Christian name and of faith. The thieves, robbers, incendiarists and murderers will not possess the kingdom of God.'[4]

Then Urban II mentions the motive which led many Christians to take part in the Crusades: the complete remission of sins. 'With willing obedience purchase for yourself the grace of God, that he may forgive you your sins with which you have aroused his wrath, for the sake of such pious works and the combined intercession of the saints. And by the mercy of God and supported by the holy apostles Peter and Paul we remit to all believing Christians who take up arms against the pagans and submit to the burden of pilgrimage all the punishment which the church has imposed on them for their sins. And if anyone fall there in true repentance, he may firmly believe that he will receive forgiveness of his sins and the fruit of eternal life.'[5]

On 15 July 1099 Jerusalem was conquered. An anonymous Chronicler reports: 'One of our men by the name of Laethold climbed on to the city wall. As soon as he succeeded, all the defenders took flight. Our people pursued them along the wall and through the city and killed and mutilated them. Then they went to the temple of Solomon; there was such a fight that we were up to our knees in the blood of our enemies . . . Soon our people ran through the city and took booty of gold, silver, horses and mules, plundering houses full of goods. Then they all assembled, full of enthusiasm and weeping for joy, at the tomb of our saviour Jesus; they worshipped and dedicated their lives to him. The next morning they quietly went on to the roof of the temple, seized the men and women of the Saracens, and cut off their heads with the naked sword.'[6]

The report of such cruel excesses of religious mania provoked sharp protests even among many Christians. Peter the Venerable, Francis of Assisi and Raymond Lull – to mention just a few – called for a peaceful mission and a literary discussion with Islam. But their appeal was drowned by the prevailing mood.

I cannot and must not go into the further history of the Crusades and the controversy with Christianity here.[7] My concern was to give an example of the way in which religious ardour, on becoming blind fanaticism, could turn into acts of bestial cruelty. This possibility alone gives us occasion to be sceptical about Christianity's claim to absoluteness.

The ideology of the Crusades manifests not least the claim of the church and the papacy to power, backed up by theology. In its name there was a call to the *militia Sancti Petri*, the holy war. Gregory VII (1037-1085), who was beatified in 1606, certainly deserves to be called the 'symbol of all the papacy's claims to absoluteness'.[8] Even if crusading fanaticism was caused to disappear because of its historical failure, this claim to power was further developed. Papal absolutism found its supreme formulation in the following four documents:

(a) The bull *Unam sanctam* of 1302 reads: 'So we declare that on pain of the loss of their souls' bliss, all human creatures must be subject to the pope in Rome, and we so say and determine.'[9] This bull was explicitly endorsed by Leo X in 1516, when the Reformation was already under way.

(b) The Council of Florence in 1441 decreed that Jesus Christ himself had given the pope the authority to lead the whole church. He was the true representative of Christ, the teacher and father of all

Christians. And the council decree then went on to state: 'No one remaining outside the Catholic Church, not just pagans, but also Jews or heretics or schismatics, can become partakers of eternal life; but they will go to the "everlasting fire which was prepared for the devil and his angels", unless before the end of life they are joined to the church.'[10]

(c) The Roman Catechism of 1566 – against the Reformers – once again strongly emphasized the sole claim of the Catholic church, its unity and uniqueness.[11] The 'Roman high priest' has legal authority given by God.[12] This marks a shift which was to shape the further development of the Roman Catholic claim to absoluteness: now it is also directed against the Reformation churches and Protestant theology, and it concentrates more and more on the pope's claim to be the divinely appointed leader of the Roman Catholic church which alone can bring salvation.

(d) This development came to an end at the First Vatican Council, at which papal infallibility (1870) was made a dogma.[13] In the *Constitutio de ecclesiae* it was declared a dogma that the pope has direct power of jurisdiction over the whole church and that the doctrinal decisions made by him *ex cathedra* are infallible. Protestant fundamentalism with its emphasis on the infallibility of the Bible is to be understood not least as a reaction against this dogma.

Solus Christus.
The Claim to Absoluteness in
Martin Luther and Karl Barth

The Reformation took shape in protest against a Roman Catholic church which had thus made itself and its supreme head absolute. Its fundamental concern was to redirect the claim to absoluteness. This was no longer to apply to the church, but to Christ alone (*solus Christus*). The ecclesiocentric claim to absoluteness (centred on the church) was to become a christocentric one (centred on Christ). Those who are fond of labels may call these two versions of the Christian claim to absoluteness 'Catholic' and 'Protestant'; however, this designation at most fits the time of the Reformation and Counter-Reformation, and even then only with qualifications.

The christocentric version immediately leads to a massive relativization of church claims to authority. It contains the ammunition for a radical criticism of the church, for an 'immanent criticism of religion'. For if we are justified by God, not as a result of our own striving to please God but only for the sake of Christ (*propter Christum*) – by grace alone (*sola gratia*) – then the whole church system of penances and indulgences is upset. The church has humbly to preach the message of the unmerited grace of God and not set itself up as the proud guardian and mediator of divine salvation. And it has constantly to allow itself to be measured in its fulfilment of this task. Christ himself is its criterion, its standard, and thus its crisis.

According to Martin Luther (1483–1546), the primary concern of the inner man is faith, not outward obedience to the church with its concern for good works and penances. So the boundary between belief and unbelief can no longer be visible, far less does it coincide with religious boundaries. The community of saints lives in the midst of a Christianity with an institutional constitution, but is not identical with it – as Augustine also thought. Thus a distinction must now be made between real (visible) and true (authentic) Christianity.

So the boundary between the word of God and the word of man no longer runs between the 'visible' Christian religion and the non-Christian religions, but between true Christianity and all that is not truly Christian, even if it has settled in the midst of visible Christianity. The absoluteness of Christianity can now no longer be understood as a given quality in this religion, a divine quality which it has come to possess, which is administered by the church with the pope at its head. At best it can exist as participation in the authority of the present Christ. Instead of *extra ecclesiam nulla salus* the saying must now run *extra Christum nulla salus*.

Different though the approaches of these two forms of the claim to absoluteness may be, they come very close in their assessment of non-Christian religions. God has made his redeeming word known for the salvation of human beings solely and only in Christ. Outside this word – *extra Christum* – there is no revelation, or at least no revelation of salvation. But where there is this revelation of salvation, where it is made present and its effective power unfolds, there true Christianity prevails. As the 'true and unique religion' (*vera et unica religio*), for Luther this true Christianity is completely different from the religion around it. The decisive difference lies in the way to salvation: the other religions seek to attain salvation through good works (self-redemption through holiness by works), whereas the Christian is justified 'by faith alone' (*sola fide* – redemption from outside by the grace of God).[1]

Luther lumps together Islam, Judaism and Catholicism ('papism') as 'religions of the law'. What they have in common is a desire to exist before God by their own effort, by their own merits. As if one could merit the forgiveness of sins and eternal life! Those who believe that, who think that they can gain God's favour by fulfilling religious and moral laws, do not take sufficiently seriously the imprisonment of men and women in their sins. Only those whom God frees from sin can exist before God. But this comes about through accepting the gospel in faith. The religion in which this happens, evangelical religion, is in principle different from other religions.

In his Greater Catechism, Luther writes in respect of the articles of faith he presents: 'Therefore these articles of faith divide and separate us Christians from all other people on earth. For whatever is outside Christianity, whether these be pagans, Turks, Jews or false Christians and hypocrites ... (will) remain in eternal wrath and damnation. For they do not have the Lord Christ, nor are they illuminated and given grace through any gifts of the Holy Spirit.'[2] The religion of the gospel contrasts with the religions of the law, as divine justification contrasts with human self-righteousness. And these forms of behaviour are related as light is to darkness. 'Where Christ is not, there is nothing but sheer idolatry, an ungodly and false notion of God, whether this be called the law of Moses, the law of the Pope or the Qur'an of the Turks.'[3]

Karl Barth (1886–1968) took up this *solus Christus* and combined it with a sharp criticism of religion, thus making Luther's approach more radical.[4] Viewed from the revelation of God in Jesus Christ, for Barth religion appears as a purely human phenomenon: as a concern for self-glorification in human beings who want to be autonomous and gain a relationship with God by their own religious efforts. Religion is the expression of a striving for self-justification and self-sanctification. Furthermore, in religion human beings even make the image of God by which they attempt to justify themselves. But because the relationship between God and human beings can only be established with an irreversible one-sidedness from God's side, any human quest for God goes against the God who seeks human beings. Religion is proud rebellion against God – not deliverance from the lostness of sins but its supreme expression: justification by works and idolatry. Thus in the light of revelation a devastating judgment is given on all religion as such: 'Religion is *unbelief*. It is a concern, indeed we must say that it is the one great concern, of *godless* man' [299f., his italics].

Here God has long since taken the decisive step towards human beings: in the event of the revelation of Christ. Human beings need only submit to this revelation; they need do nothing towards it, they can and may do nothing towards it if they do not want to fail in the relationship opened up by God.

No religion, even the Christian religion, is true in itself. The only truth, outside which there can be only lies, falsehood and injustice before God, is and remains God's word itself [325]. In stubborn opposition to revelation, in living and teaching with self-certainty in its own power, the Christian religion stands alongside all other religions in the solidarity of sin.

But out of his incomprehensible grace God has chosen this one religion to be the vessel of his truth; he has forgiven its sin, justified it and hallowed it. By linking it with the name of Jesus Christ, the embodiment and source of all reality [345 and 348], he has elevated it to be the true religion and thus given it the right of firstborn among the religions [334]. As the religion created, chosen, justified and hallowed by God, Christianity is 'different and separate from all other religions' [358]. All its doctrines and forms of life are beyond comparison with their non-Christian counterparts.

Certainly Barth never wearies of emphasizing that this gift of grace is beyond human control, is a completely unmerited gift; he even emphasizes that there is nothing in Christianity itself which could make it worthy of this designation. On the contrary, it too is and always remains unbelief, just as the justified sinner also still remains a sinner. But he can similarly allow that the sole, exclusive truth of God has manifested itself in Christianity and nowhere else. As a hallowed religion, representing revelation, Christianity is no longer on a level with or even a stage above the other religions, but is as qualitatively different from them as light from darkness and truth from the lie [346f.]. It has been snatched 'like a brand from the burning', from 'the world of religions and the judgment and sentence pronounced on them' [356]. As an embodiment of the message of Christ it can lay claim to uniqueness, once-for-allness and exclusivity. Elevated by God to be a powerful announcement of his revelation, it can now encounter the religions in unbroken self-consciousness [331–3], and in a mission authenticated by God invite them to return to the Christian way [356f.]. Though Barth warns against translating the divine verdict that religion is unbelief into human condemnations, it stands as a divine verdict on the religions.

So two answers are to be given to the question of Christianity's claim to absoluteness: 1. Christianity is absolute (in the sense of unique) as the true religion vouchsafed by God. 2. However, the truth of God is a gift of God beyond human control from which nothing can be subtracted by human disputes and to which nothing can be added by human assertions and justifications. Where the Christian religion claims this absoluteness for itself, where on the basis of its religious qualities it strives for pre-eminence among the other religions, it is subjected to harsh criticism. Precisely in entering into competition with the other religions and thus being concerned to demonstrate its superiority by commending its own strength, it degrades itself to becoming a mere religious association which in principle is on the same level as other religious structures and in so doing denies its right as firstborn among the religions [334, 294].

Certainly the revelation of Christ elevates the church to the status of the true religion, but it does not give it this title to possess. It prevents Christianity from identifying itself with the truth which it incorporates and claiming absolute validity. Thus the absoluteness of Christianity is on the one hand conceded, but on the other is left pending as something which has merely been lent.

Barth's verdict for decades disqualified the concept and reality of religion in German-speaking Protestantism, and resulted in a widespread ignorance of the study of religions. Only at the end of the 1960s and the beginning of the 1970s did a new move to the religions begin. We shall be returning to this in the last chapter.

13

The Other Way: Inclusive Absoluteness

If we survey the milestones in the development of the Christian claim to absoluteness as they have been described so far, it may seem that the only reaction of Christianity to other religions was to assert itself by separation. But this picture is a one-sided one. At all times in the history of the church and theology, alongside the definitions and structures which set the church apart there was also a tradition of association. The term inclusiveness has come to be used for this, in contrast to the exclusiveness that we have come across so far. I shall now compare the inclusive and exclusive attitudes as types, in order to work out some of their important characteristics, and then pursue the inclusive line through some of its important stages in history.

The exclusive (or monopolistic) claim to absoluteness asserts the that Christianity alone is valid. Emphasis is put on its incomparable uniqueness – what in principle distinguishes it from other religions. In such uniqueness it is absolute, i.e. detached from anything that might seem similar to it.

Thus for example Christianity is said to be incomparable with other religions because it is not a religion. As we saw, this is the line that Barth took. Its core is revelation, not religious practice; God's self-disclosure for human salvation, not the human quest for God. Or the religion of the gospel is diametrically opposed to another religion of the law, as happens with Luther: human beings are redeemed from outside by God's unmerited grace, not by themselves through their own efforts at piety.

It thus becomes clear, time and again, that where exclusive claims to absoluteness are made there is often a dualistic thought-pattern in the background: true–untrue, right–wrong, *religio vera – religio falsa*, light and darkness, good and evil, election and rejection, redemption and lostness, grace and judgment, salvation and damnation, heaven and hell, the grace of God and human works, God and Satan. There is only an either–or: nothing in between. The ungodly, untruth, is to be fought against, and the divine, the truth, is to be carried into the world through mission. Here the notion of God's judgment plays an important part in the background.

By contrast, the inclusive claim to absoluteness does not affirm the sole validity of Christianity but its qualitative superiority to the other religions. Whereas according to the exclusive model these are rejected uncompromisingly – as darkness, as blasphemous heresy, as the work of the Antichrist – they are now given a degree of positive value. Individual rays of the divine light have also appeared in them and have shed light on them. Thus it can be explained that a form of belief in God can also be found in them, or at least that there are also virtuous people beyond the limits of Christianity.

The sparks of truth scattered in the non-Christian religions are not excluded from God's action of revelation and salvation (that would be the 'exclusive' position), but included in this action (hence the description 'inclusive' model). They are related to Christianity (or the message of Christ) as plan to fulfilment, part to whole, seed to plant.

To justify this view one could refer to those passages in the Bible which speak of a universal primal revelation of God to all human beings, above all Romans 1.18–20 and 2.14f., but also John 1.9; Acts 14.15–17 and 17.22–31. This idea can be combined with the Stoic notion that *all* human beings are endowed with the natural light of reason (what Cicero calls the *lumen naturale*) and so in principle are also capable of knowing God. Such a relatively positive estimate of the human capacity for reason makes it possible to replace the exclusive dualism of light and darkness – truth here and untruth there – with an inclusive two-stage theory: perfect, pure truth here and fragmentary truth mixed with untruth there.

This model leads to an ambivalent assessment of the religions: viewed positively, they are preliminary stages, a preparation for the gospel. They prepare for the reception of the message of Christ. And conversely, where this message goes forth, it can take up the elements of truth contained in the religions. Negatively, the religions are disturbances, obscurings, fragments, distortions of the one truth which God has revealed in Christ.

The religions need not be condemned as heresy, but can be recognized positively – only, however, as preliminary stages, as partial truths, as approaches to Christ. Christ is the goal, the end and the consummation of all religions. Though fragments of God's truth may be found in the religions, the whole and perfect truth of God lies only in Christ. And *the* religion which is illuminated by this truth stands above all other religions. All the truths that may be contained in them are sublated and surpassed here; 'sublated' in the threefold sense in which Hegel uses the word: ended (*negare*), preserved (*conservare*) and raised to a higher level (*levare*).

The non-Christian religions have a right to exist, but only until the Christian message reaches them. Then their fate, which has already long been sealed, is decided: they must come to Christ or give way to him.

The two forms of the claim to absoluteness – the exclusive, monopolistic one and the inclusive, superior one – correspond directly to two patterns of behaviour towards non-Christian forms of belief and their adherents. The exclusive definition of the relationship calls for strict separation from other religions, for their repudiation and for an attempt to convert their adherents to the true faith. Non-Christian religion is branded an error which leads to the abyss of irrevocable lostness. This error must be sharply repudiated, and those on the way to it must be rescued from danger.

By contrast, the definition of an inclusive relationship seeks the sparks of truth in the other faith which can positively meet up with the message of Christ. It is a call to preserve the good things of this faith but to go beyond them, and in this way to attain to the fullness of salvation in Jesus Christ, to the complete, full, perfect truth.

I shall call the pattern of behaviour produced by the exclusive definition of relationship the exclusion or repudiation model and that produced by the inclusive attitude the integration, association or assimilation model. The two patterns lead to characteristically different mission strategies.

According to the association model, those of another faith can be regarded as potential Christians. That being so, it must be the aim of Christian mission to make these potential Christians actual Christians. Here it is important to seek positive points of contact in active friendship with them: for example, ethical principles which resemble

Christian principles; experiences of life which can be seen as religious and can be illuminated by the gospel; traces of the activity of God in their lives. The preacher will take up such approaches and translate the message of Christ in terms of the background disclosed in this way.

By contrast, the repudiation model is committed to the discovery of erroneous belief, demonstrating its real basis and pronouncing a verdict on it. Non-Christians have to leave their false ways and repent, i.e. be converted.

Often one model runs directly into the other: in the eyes of the missionary, those who regard the friendliness with which they are wooed as excessive boldness and reject it are demonstrating their stubbornness. Then the missionary concern to rescue them can easily turn into a battle against their unbelief: 'So you don't want to be our brothers and sisters . . .'

Of course we can ask whether the 'soft', inclusive claim to superiority may be understood as a claim to absoluteness at all. Is not that term better reserved for the 'hard' claims to exclusiveness? However, if we consider how the inclusive view has a tendency to commandeer, such doubts quickly subside. Quite apart from this, numerous advocates of this line explicitly make claims about the absoluteness of Christianity.

The universalistic inclusive approach was first developed into a doctrine when the Christian religion, still young, extended beyond the cultural sphere of Palestine. In the world of Hellenistic thought it encountered not only the religious syncretism described above, but also the great tradition of Greek philosophy: Socrates, Plato and Aristotle. Could these great thinkers have had such spiritual achievements had not 'divine light' shone on them? It was the same with the Old Testament prophets and Abraham and Moses. After all, they too had been sent by God and were righteous in his sight – *before* Christ!

In order to be able to understand these two pre-Christian currents of truth – the history of the Greek spirit and the history of the Jewish experience of God – as prehistories of Christianity, Justin Martyr (who died around 165) developed the doctrine of the 'seeds of truth' (of the Logos[1]), the *logoi spermatikoi*, which God had scattered in rational souls. On entering the human world the seeds of truth were taken over by the false and the demonic. In the revelation of Christ these pre-Christian, tainted particles of truth find the fulfilment and consummation for which they are meant from the start. For in Christ the Logos who scattered the seeds of truth appeared in fullness and purity; here he became man.[2] Thus Justin can say: 'Christ was and is the Logos who dwells in *every* man.'[3] And: '*All* the human race has a portion in Christ, God's firstborn.'[4]

The appearance of the Logos in Christ is unsurpassable. There can never be a more complete revelation. Anyone who knows and believes this is in God's truth, is truly a Christian. However, all those who lived *before* Christ 'in accord with the Logos'[5] are also Christians (of a lesser degree of purity).[5] Whatever has been aptly said by Stoics, poets and writers 'belongs to us Christians'.[6]

This phrase 'belongs to us Christians' further explains why one may speak of assimilation here. The non-Christian truth is incorporated into the Christian truth, taken into it, absorbed by it.

Even Tertullian, who repudiated Greek philosophy so sharply, knows of the capacity of all human beings to see the (manifest) truth of the Christian faith. For a disposition towards the truth has been implanted in the soul which has been created by God and is therefore 'naturally Christian'.[7]

Clement of Alexandria, who died some time after 215, took up the Logos doctrine and developed it into a comprehensive theology of history. In it, Greek philosophy has the role of a 'tutor to Christ' and of a 'second testament' alongside the Old Testament.[8] Its task is to educate humankind to Christ.

Augustine also expressed the view that the truth of God was already known before Christ: 'For what is now called the Christian religion already existed among the ancients, indeed it has not been absent since the beginning of the human race, until Christ himself appeared in the flesh. From then the true religion which had always existed began to be called Christian.'[9]

And even at the time of the Crusades – as we saw above – voices were not lacking which protested against the condemnation of pagans and Jews. This was not only because the atrocities committed were a slap in the face for universal Christian ethics, but also because the theological judgment on Jews and pagans which lay behind them contradicted the view of humanity held by many spokesmen of mediaeval Christianity. Mention should be made here primarily of Abelard (1079–1142) with his dispositional ethic: in his view, anyone who acts to the best of his knowledge and conscience remains guiltless even if his conscience is wrong. Now if guilt presupposes an evil intent, then ignorant pagans are guiltless. Furthermore, on the basis of their special illuminations the great sages of antiquity could even attain to knowledge of divine truth, so that they are to be regarded as Christians even if they knew nothing of Christ.[10]

The combination of nature and grace as two storeys one above the other also allowed Thomas Aquinas (1225–1274) to speak of an implicit faith in Christ among all those who know God from creation by the natural light of reason and who live in accordance with his will, i.e. morally.[11] Supernature, the divine illumination through revelation, does not eliminate rational human nature but picks it up, takes it beyond itself and completes it.[12]

This 'two-storey' model can lead to openness to the truth-claims made by other religions without damaging the uniqueness of Christianity. As the one and only religion endowed with the revelation of Christ, Christianity does not compare with the other 'natural' religions as light with darkness but as the destination with the way, the achievement with the plan. Certainly the plan cannot be completed without a *break*; it calls for repentance. But this repentance need not involve the repudiation of all pre-Christian truth-claims. For 'every truth, by whomever it may be said, is from the Holy Spirit in the sense that he imparts the natural light of reason and that he moves the mind to understand and utter the truth'.[13]

So the concession that there can also be authentic (though not complete) knowledge of God outside the revelation of Christ is directly connected with a positive assessment of rational human nature. But where this nature is said to have been radically corrupted, because it is totally fallen, the necessary consequence must be a strictly exclusive claim for the message of Christ as the medium of the knowledge of God, as we have seen in the cases of both Luther and Barth.

The scholastic theologians of the Middle Ages had above all the Greek philosophers in mind when they conceded the possibility of divine revelations to the pagans. They taught that God had illuminated individual 'holy pagans' with his grace. Nicolas of Cusa (1401–1464) goes an important stage beyond this and makes an attempt which is revolutionary for his time to give a quite positive evaluation of the other religions. He believes that 'God is sought in the different religions in different ways and given different names'.[14] For centuries this notion made no impact at all on the official teaching of the Catholic church.

Only in the Second Vatican Council (1962–1965) was there an epoch-making opening up of the Catholic church to the other religions. Whereas earlier it had been said that those who are not Christians can be justified *despite* their (false) religion, now this religion appeared, if not as a way to God, at least as an expression of worthwhile truth. 'The Catholic Church rejects nothing of what is true and holy in these religions. She has a high regard for the manner of life and conduct, the precepts and doctrines which, although differing in many ways from her own teaching, nevertheless often reflect a ray of that truth which enlightens all men.'[15] Then the council document goes on to describe such 'rays of truth' in the religions: the Muslims – to take just this one example – are deeply respected because they 'worship God, who is one, living and subsistent, merciful and almighty, the Creator of heaven and earth', and because the Qur'an reveres Abraham, Jesus and Mary and teaches fear of the day of judgment. So the former hostility to Muslims must be buried in order to join common cause with them for 'peace and freedom for all peoples'.[16]

But despite all this, the claim of Christianity to absoluteness remains unaffected: the preamble to the Declaration on Religious Liberty runs: 'The sacred Council begins by professing that God himself has made known to the human race how men by serving him can be saved and reach happiness in Christ. We believe that this one true religion continues to exist in the Catholic and Apostolic Church, to which the Lord Jesus entrusted the task of spreading it among all men.'[17]

Karl Rahner (1908–1984) even ventured to go a step further and recognized the non-Christian religions as relatively valid ways to truth.[18] He was deeply convinced of God's will for universal salvation: God cannot allow anyone to be excluded from salvation. So for him grace is not set above nature as a second storey but is implanted in human nature itself in the form of a 'supernatural existential'. In other words, all people are by nature dependent on God's grace, and thus on Jesus Christ as the complete form of this grace. If people intuitively follow the direction of their innermost aim, they are Christians, even if they do not consciously believe in Christ. So there is a pre-conscious gift of grace, an 'implicit faith', an 'anonymous Christianity'.

The non-Christian religions can be seen as social forms of anonymous Christianity. In them human beings can encounter God's grace; therein lies their legitimacy. However, if the message of Christ reaches anonymous Christians and commits them existentially, then they face the decision of either rejecting his salvation or becoming confessing Christians. Both anonymous Christianity and the legitimacy of the non-Christian religions end at this threshold. So even Rahner does not take back the monopoly of salvation in Christ – represented in his church.

The current position of the Roman Catholic church on this question is laid down in the document *Dialogue and Proclamation. Reflections and Guidelines on Inter-religious Dialogue and the Proclamation of the Gospel of Jesus Christ*, published by the Papal Council for Inter-religious Dialogue and the Congregation for the Evangelization of the Nations, and dated 19 May 1991. This states: ' . . . the adherents of other religions always give a positive response to God's invitation and receive his salvation in Jesus Christ if they honestly put into practice the good contained in their traditions and follow the dictates of their consciences. This applies even if they do not recognize or acknowledge Jesus Christ as their saviour.' In other words, God also brings about his salvation – which is always the salvation present in Jesus Christ – in non-Christian religions.

This sketch of some theological positions which are conceived after the model of inclusive universalism indicates that the claim of Christianity to absoluteness need not assume an exclusive and separatist form but can also be combined with a generous recognition of non-Christian claims to truth. But it is always the *Christian* truths that are recognized in others, as they (or something similar) are found. Religious convictions are not understood as the adherents of the religions themselves understand them, but as they correspond to Christian faith, detached from the overall framework of the particular religion and 'forcibly baptized'. One is reminded of those who judge all that they encounter abroad by the standards of what they are familiar with at home.

14

The Absoluteness of Christianity and the History of Religion

A brief retrospect. From the beginning of the Middle Ages to the Enlightenment the non-Christian religions did not really raise any questions for the truth-claim of Christianity. The truth revealed by God was contained in the Bible. The religion founded on it was the true religion, so all other religions – if they were to be called religions at all – had to be false. It could be conceded that there had also been 'holy pagans' in these religions, but they were holy not as a result of, but despite, their religion. With God, nothing was impossible, even for him to proclaim his truth in a miraculous way to pagans. There was no doubt about the falsehood of the religions in which they lived.

Even when the early Enlightenment developed its theory of natural religion (i.e. religion given naturally to all human beings as rational beings), nothing changed here. Certainly now all 'positive' religions (i.e. religions which could be found in history – Judaism, Christianity, Islam, etc.) were given priority and thus Christianity was to some degree relativized. But the demonstration that the Christian religion of revelation corresponded to the religion of reason had shown its truth and its pre-eminence: the non-Christian religions appeared as corrupt forms of natural religion and Christianity as its full realization.

When the idea of natural religion faced a crisis (with David Hume), the Christian religion suddenly found itself put as religion on a level with the other religions: as one of several religions in the stream of the general history of religion. The summary subordination of religions to the general term religion put them all side by side as species of the same genre. Thus for the first time for many centuries Christianity was put in a competitive situation not only on the periphery but also in its heartlands. Not *de facto*, by the attack of alien religions, but – far worse – theologically, from within and not from outside.

Gotthold Ephraim Lessing's (1729–1781) parable of the rings marked the end of the absoluteness of Christianity based on the theology of revelation. He thought the dispute between Jews, Christians and Muslims over the true religion impossible to resolve in his time: only 'over thousands upon thousands of years'[1] would it prove which was the true religion – by its influence. This deprived the Christian truth-claim of a validity that had been taken for granted. But what about the uniqueness of Christianity, its special position and superiority?

Friedrich Schleiermacher (1768–1834) and Georg Friedrich Wilhelm Hegel (1770–1831) were the first to accept this challenge. In order to demonstrate the superiority of Christianity over the other religions, they developed the self-understanding of Christian faith in a comparison with these religions. Set in the world of religions, Christianity now had to demonstrate its special character in order to back up its claim to truth. A simple reference to the authority of revelation was no longer convincing. There was need of a historical and philosophical proof to back up the uniqueness of this one religion. Essentially there were two stages to this.

First of all the 'essence of religion' (i.e. the universal goal of all religions) was defined. This was found in the reconciliation of God and humankind. Christianity with its doctrine of the incarnation of God could then – and this is the second stage – be regarded as the perfect realization of this goal. According to Schleiermacher, Christianity is thus 'the religion of religions', because here religion has realized itself – in the perfect mediation between the infinite and the finite.

This gave birth to efforts to demonstrate that Christianity was the 'absolute religion'.[2] In this context people began to talk about the 'absoluteness of Christianity'. So this is where the history of this term has its origin. The context is one in which a claim to the absoluteness of Christianity which had previously been based on the authority of revelation was in crisis, where people attempted to overcome this crisis by attempting to vindicate the pre-eminence of Christianity from a comparison of religions. I cannot describe the whole history of these attempts, nor is that my concern, so I shall merely single out its climax, which is also its conclusion, Ernst Troeltsch's *The Absoluteness of Christianity and the History of Religion*, which appeared in 1902.[3]

Ernst Troeltsch (1865–1923) saw very clearly that consistently historical thought which understands history as an ongoing complex without special spheres that can be detached cannot absolutize a particular religion, i.e. extract it from its context. To the degree that the traditional assertions of the absoluteness of Christianity did precisely this, this approach took the ground from under them. The Christian religion must be put in the general history of religion without any reservations. It cannot claim absolute and unparalleled uniqueness any more than it can claim final validity and universality. 'It is impossible to construct a theory of Christianity as the absolute religion on the basis of a historical way of thinking or by the use of historical means' [63].

However, its relative pre-eminence can be demonstrated, as a religion among religions. For a comparison to be possible, a criterion, a standard is needed. For Troeltsch this standard consists in the departure of a religion from any roots in the world or nature (including natural human capacities). The more spiritual a religion is, the more a 'higher, spiritual and eternal world' 'of absolutely transcendent religious values' [109] is opposed to the natural world of the senses, the higher the value embodied in it. The more a religion regards God and human beings as free personalities which shape the world, the higher validity this religion has.

The so-called natural religions – Troeltsch calls them the 'polytheisms and polydemonisms of the lower stages' [108] – *a priori* differ from this. According to Troeltsch, religions of the law – like Judaism and Islam – are inferior to the religions of redemption because while they divide the two worlds – the natural and the spiritual – they expect an upward ascent to be made by human beings themselves (i.e. with the natural power of their souls). By contrast, in the religions of redemption the soul is freed from its own nature, fills itself solely with the forces of the divine and plays a formative role in the world in which it is set, realizing absolute values [108]. In addition to Christianity, Troeltsch includes in this group of religions in particular the religions of India, by which he understands

Brahmanism (Hinduism) and Buddhism. But even in these two Far Eastern religions it is ultimately human beings themselves who have to work out their redemption, not by observing the law but by gaining great spiritual depth and withdrawing from a world which is only one of appearances; so here, too, influence from the natural religions forces its way through [110f.]. Thus according to Troeltsch, the Eastern religions do not really do justice to the concept of the religion of redemption. He finds a further deficiency in the 'mystical' it-ness, impersonality and lack of historicity in their picture of God. The deity is not regarded in personal terms but as a reified It which rests in itself and outside the world [111]. So at the end of the comparison of religions Christianity may receive the crown: it is the 'strongest and most concentrated revelation of personalistic religious apprehension' [112], a collection of all religious values and thus the most intensive of the world religions.

In this way once again we encounter the contrast between two ways to redemption which we already met in Luther: self-redemption from the natural human powers of body and soul on the one hand and redemption from outside by the revelation of a spiritual word beyond the senses on the other.

The problems in this scheme are obvious: the criterion by which religions are measured is derived from Christianity – or, more precisely, from Central European Christianity at the turn of the century. And because the whole comparison of religions is already decided by the choice of the criterion, it is clear *a priori* that Christianity must be superior to all other religions. The value judgment of the Christian who is making the decision is presented as the result of a scientific comparison.

Yet here an attempt has been made to begin not from a theological pre-judgment on religions but from the reality of religions in history. We cannot go back behind this step if we are interested in an authentic dialogical relationship. But we must attempt even more strongly than Troeltsch did to understand the religions from within, in terms of their own self-understanding, if we are really to do them justice.

With this thought I want to bring our journey through church history and theology to an end. It should have become clear how many different courses Christianity can adopt in differentiating itself from non-Christian religions. What form of claim to absoluteness Christianity makes depends not least on the particular situation and on the personality profiles of individual Christians.

However, I must dwell on Troeltsch for a moment longer. For not only did he make his own attempt to demonstrate the 'relative absoluteness' of Christianity from the history of religion; he also (influenced by Schleiermacher) developed an important approach towards interpreting this claim to absoluteness. At the centre of this interpretation is the distinction between natural (or naive, i.e. pre-reflective) and artificial absoluteness.

Troeltsch sees the source of any claim to religious absoluteness in the encounter with the Absolute itself, in the experience of God. This 'natural' experience of the Absolute takes place with the immediately compelling certainty of having recognized the 'final and absolute truth' [157]. Where this original experience of certainty is intellectualized, where it is channelled into apologetic and dogmatic principles, an 'artificial' claim to absoluteness arises. Accordingly, the Christian claim to absoluteness is the result of a process of coagulation, in which an original experience of being grasped by the Absolute is fossilized in theological notions and doctrines for which an unconditional claim to validity is made.

Karl Jaspers (1883–1969) takes a quite similar direction in his ideas about the Christian claim to absoluteness.[4] He distinguishes between existential and rational truth. The truths of faith are existential, not rational truths. The correctness of rational truth can be proved, since it is 'universally valid, unhistorical, timeless, but not unconditional' [11]. By contrast, human beings live by existential truth; it 'is only by my becoming identical with it; it is historical in its manifestation, not universal in its objective expressibility, but it is unconditional' [11]. Where a claim is made for a content to faith which only has the universal validity and exclusiveness of scientific knowledge, i.e. where there is a 'transformation of the unconditional nature of existential resolve into a knowledge of what is right' [70f.], religious claims to absoluteness come into being. Thus they are expressions of a narrowing down of existential truth to rational correctness [11, 70f.].

The interpretation of Gustav Mensching (1901–1978) is also

closely related to that of Troeltsch and Jaspers. Mensching sees the claim to absoluteness arising on the threshold between 'intensive' experience and 'extensive' assertion. 'Intensive absoluteness' as an expression of a personal tie to God is necessarily exclusive, since this relationship to God radically excludes other religious ties.[5] But it is highly personal and not universal. Now if this certainty overreaches itself by combining itself with the claim to be the only binding religion of all human beings, the intensive experience becomes an 'extensive claim to absoluteness'.[6] According to Mensching, too, the claim to absoluteness produces an inappropriate generalization: the uninterrupted transference of the personal conviction of faith to the level of universal validity. So according to Mensching, the extensive claim to absoluteness is 'to be rejected as a distortion of what was originally meant'.[7]

Ernst Troeltsch, Karl Jaspers and Gustav Mensching explain the rise of religious claims to absoluteness in terms of a consolidation of the original religious certainty of the truth. Their criticism is directed against the generalization of certainties which cannot be generalized. The unconditional existential truth can only be relational, i.e. related to the person who experiences it.[8]

One is reminded of Dostoievsky's legend of the Grand Inquisitor. In his conversation with Christ, the Inquisitor says: 'For the chief concern of those miserable creatures is not only to find something that I or someone else can worship, but to find something that all beings can worship, and the absolutely essential thing is that they should do so *all together*. It is this need for *universal* worship that is the chief torment of every man individually and of mankind as a whole from the beginning of time. For the sake of that universal worship they have put each other to the sword.'[9]

Before we come to the question where (and in what way) this claim to absoluteness is an indispensable element of Christian faith, in the next chapter I want to broaden our horizons and investigate the degree to which some of the great non-Christian religions separate themselves from other religions.

15

Claims to Absoluteness in the Religions

If we adopt the typology of Friedrich Heiler, and understand the religions coming from India as mystical and those from the Semitic sphere as prophetic,[1] then (to simplify crudely) we can say that claims to absoluteness flourish more in prophetic than in mystical religions. The religions of Semitic origin (Judaism, Christianity and Islam) provide essentially more fertile soil for the 'absolutist' attitudes than religions of Indian origin (Hinduism[2] and Buddhism).

Certainly there are also fundamentalist movements in religions of Indian origin, though these are constantly said to be tolerant through and through and resistant to all fundamentalist temptations.

At the latest since the brutal disputes over the holy place in Ayodhiya in North India to which both Muslims and Hindus laid claim, we have been made vividly aware of this fact. After fundamentalist Hindus destroyed the Babri mosque to build a temple to Rama on the site, bloody battles broke out betwen Hindus and Muslims which spilled over to other places and cost the lives of hundreds of people. The National Voluntary Aid Corps and the nationalistic Hindu Shiv Sena (Shiva's army) call for the submission of all religions and minorities to the Hindu majority. The Bharata Janata Party is politically on the increase and has already seized power in some areas of India. Bairang Dal, the youth organization of Vishwa Hindu Parishad, with a strict Hindu orientation, has called for a holy war against the Muslims.[3]

However, we should see such phenomena more as the use of Indian religion as a political instrument than as its genuine expression. The basic attitude of these religions, their relationship to the divine, to history and to other religions, makes the formation of 'absolutist' attitudes difficult, rather than encouraging them.

For the mystical religions know the divine less as a person who leads his people through history than as the infinite, timeless ground of being resting on itself, the Absolute. It is history that has to be overcome. The goal is the redemption of the world by entering into this sea of being. 'The basic experience of mystical piety is the denial of the vital instincts, a renunciation and dissolution of the human, a dedication to infinity, which climaxes in ecstasy or nirvana. Mystical piety is thus primarily turned inwards; it strives to be free from desire, to extinguish affective and volitional life . . . The high point of a life of mystical piety is reached in extraordinary experience beyond normal consciousness: new dimensions of perception and discernment, ecstasies and ecstasy-like visions and hearing of voices . . .'[4] The danger in this basic attitude lies in its turning away from the world, in its attitude of cosmic indifference.

By contrast, prophetic piety is directed towards God as the initiator of history. Without issuing in history, it intervenes actively in it, with the goal of bringing in the kingdom of God. The revelation of God has historical gravity; it is attached to particular historical events (the Exodus from Egypt, the Christ event, the prophecy of Muhammad) and media (holy scriptures) and thus absolutizes these events and media as spheres of events and bearers of revelation. However, here also lies the great danger of all prophetic religion; it tends more towards the objectification of the presence of God, towards the binding of the Spirit which blows where it wills to the media through which it works (or has worked). Veneration of holy scriptures is the best example of this.

Where the adherents of the prophetic religions bind God's dynamic presence in the Spirit exclusively and absolutely to his manifestations and thus reify them, and where the manifestations lose their character as a mediator with God and themselves become the object of divine veneration, they are in danger of becoming idols. The divinization of things and events within history easily leads to the divine being made finite.[5] And the exclusivist assertion that God has revealed himself here and only here, which is characteristic of the claim to absoluteness, is involved in this danger of what Rosemary Ruether calls 'incarnationalism'.

'The basic experience of prophetic piety . . . is characterized by a strong will to live: an instinct for affirmation, a condition in which one is gripped by values and responsibilities, a passionate striving for the realization of certain goals and ideals. Prophetic piety is thus primarily turned outwards, stands up to confront the world, and aims to prevail in it.'[6]

The adherents of a prophetic religion see themselves under pressure to decide; they must not only prove their faith in shaping the world but also constantly ward off attacks by that which is opposed to God, since they are engaged in a cosmic confrontation. Here the uniqueness of life in a time that is running out also creates additional pressure (in contrast to the idea of reincarnation in Indian religions, with their infinite cyclical view of time). Eternal life or eternal damnation is decided on the basis of a brief life on earth.

I now want to investigate the individual religions to see whether and to what extent they offer favourable conditions for the growth of claims to absoluteness on the basis of their origins.

Judaism and Islam

Where a people not only claims uniqueness and exclusiveness for its God, but also claims to be the people chosen by this God, the door has manifestly been opened to religious self-absolutizing. Strict monotheism (Isa.44.6) was (and is) combined among the Jews with a consciousness of election – a combination which almost of necessity led to a claim to absoluteness for their own religion. In an 'almost rabid intolerance'[7] the God of Israel forbids 'his' people to have dealings with other gods and to take other ways of salvation. Here is one of the most important roots of the claims to exclusiveness in all three Abrahamic religions.

God had 'called' this people Israel and 'separated' them from the nations to be 'his' people. As a 'holy' people it is his special possession (Deut.7.6; 14.2). Moreover, the Jews also constantly made a fundamental distinction between themselves and the Goyim, the peoples, the Gentiles. However much the people of God is to shine out on the nations, it is to protect itself from pagan influences. Already in a very old saying, Balaam the seer remarks: 'Lo, a people dwelling alone, and not reckoning itself among the nations' (Num.23.9). After the Babylonian exile, in his fight to distinguish Israel from other peoples, Ezra went so far as to call for the dissolution of mixed marriages.

But precisely where there was a move towards making the religion absolute, with a reference to election, prophets emerged to attack such self-satisfaction. They recalled that election is not primarily a special mark of divine approval, a privilege and a blessing, but a strict obligation. God expected Israel, the people whom he had chosen, also to choose him – not just with lip service but with acts of righteousness within and with active witness to the glory of God to outsiders. So the election of this people is not unconditional, but always has a condition attached to it. 'If you will obey my voice and keep my covenant, you shall be my own possession among all peoples' (Ex.19.5).

Where the elect people does not fulfil this special responsibility, it will be called to account by its God in a special way: 'You alone have I known of all the families of the earth; therefore I will punish you for all your iniquities' (Amos 3.2). Where Israel retreated into its special status before God and forgot the obligation which went with it, it was immediately denied this status and found itself put amongst the peoples: 'Are you not like the Ethiopians to me, O people of Israel?' says the Lord. 'Did I not bring up Israel from the land of Egypt, and the Philistines from Caphtor and the Syrians from Kir?' (Amos 9.7; 6.1f.).[8] Any withdrawal from responsibility before God immediately leads to God's withdrawal from a people which is glorifying itself. Anyone who wanted to make a claim to absoluteness for Judaism as a religion was fundamentally going against the heart of this religion.

The later prophets who stood under the shadow of the Bablyonian exile emphasized the universality of the divine will for salvation: that God has a special relationship to Israel does not mean that he has no relationship to the other peoples. In Israel God's light is to shine out for the nations (Isa.42.6; 49.6; 51.4). This takes up the promise that at the end of time the nations will stream to Zion as the place of God's revelation (Isa.2.1–4; Micah 4.1–5). The goal of Israel's election is universal: salvation for the nations.

But that does not mean that all the nations are to convert to Judaism. A universal task of mission is completely alien to this religion. 'Judaism does not have the ambition to save humankind because it has never claimed that humankind is lost without it. Judaism claims that as far as non-Jews are concerned, the righteous among all the peoples will have a share in the world to come.'[9]

With this consciousness of the universality of God's activity, Jews could even recognize the wisdom proclaimed in other religions, as the following prayer from the liturgy of Reform Judaism – based on a Talmudic blessing – indicates: 'We give thanks for the sages and teachers of all peoples and faiths who have brought many to a deeper understanding of You and Your will.'[10]

'Judaism has the great good fortune to have brought two daughter religions into the world under God. But the same Judaism has the problem that as soon as the two daughters became theologically autonomous and parted company with their mother, they regarded themselves as the perfection and crown of Judaism and in so doing really wrote Judaism off as a museum piece.'[11] The relationship between the daughters and the mother is determined by their claim to have the final and concluding revelation. This claim to finality was made both by Christianity against Judaism – as we saw in Chapter 7 – and also by Islam against Judaism and Christianity.

Whereas the Jews regarded God's history with their people as one open to fulfilment (which *a priori* took the ground from under any claims to finality), Christians and Muslims see the decisive event in history as already having come. Just as Christians worship Christ as the definitive word of God become man, so for Muslims the Qur'an is the final word of God revealed through the prophet Muhammad. 'This book is not to be doubted. It is a guide to the righteous' (2.2[12]). The Qur'an makes the claim that Islam is the only true religion before God;[13] anyone who does not accept it is lost;[14] and anyone who opposes it must be fought against (8.39f.; 9.29–35; 2.192–194). Muhammad appears as the 'seal of the prophets' (33.41), i.e., with his revelation the history of revelation has reached its final conclusion, which cannot be surpassed.

However, this does not amount to an exclusive claim against its predecessors Judaism and Christianity which denies these religions their character as revelation and condemns them. Islam confronts these 'religions of the book' with the inclusive claim that it is the completion of their revelation.

Where the Qur'an criticizes Jews and Christians, this is not (according to Islamic self-understanding) a criticism of the revelations and the prophetic revealers of these religions but a criticism of those adherents who (from the perspective of Islam) have deviated from their own revelations. Underlying these statements are experiences which Muhammad had with neighbouring Jews and Christians. These were peripheral groups which had already moved a long way from the mainstream of their faith communities: Jewish tribes which no longer embodied Torah Judaism, and heretical Christians: Nestorians, Monophysites and Jewish–Christian Gnostics.[15]

So Islam does not reject the revelations and prophets to which Jews and Christians refer. On the contrary, it accepts their validity (2.137) and claims to renew them in their original meaning. For Islam does not understand itself as a new revelation which came into the world with Muhammad (46.10), but as the age-old, original, one and only religion which was given to all human beings from the beginning of creation. Both the Jewish Torah and the Christian gospel proclaim this one religion and are therefore 'sent by God' (2.137; 4.164f.; 5.45–49). But because these revelations were subsequently changed by their adherents, they no longer correspond to the original heavenly writing (2.76f.; 5.15ff.). So God felt the need to hand down a new, authentic copy of the original document. But that does not alter the fact that by virtue of their revelations and their prophets Judaism and Christianity are 'an essential ingredient of the Islamic way of salvation'.[16]

H. Stieglecker has summed up what the Qur'an says about the relationship between the three revealed writings like this:[17] '1. All three are "books of God" which were "sent down" by God to Moses, Jesus and Muhammad; God's word is in each of them. 2. The Jews and Christians who received the Torah and Gospel through Moses or Jesus are obliged to observe the laws of these holy books and to be governed by them. Anyone who does not observe them is an unbeliever, unrighteous, wicked. Similarly, even Muhammad is enjoined to observe the Qur'an. 3. Torah, Gospel and Qu'ran are accordingly sent by God; as such they cannot contradict one another, but rather confirm one another. That is a fact to which the Qur'an constantly points. The Torah is confirmed by the Gospel as having been sent by God, and Torah and Gospel are confirmed by the Qur'an as books of God ... And on the other hand the Qur'an is proclaimed in advance by Torah and Gospel as the book of God, as that book of God which, having been sent to the last prophet, is the completion of all that is sent down. That is the express teaching of the Qur'an. 4. Because Torah, Gospel and Qur'an contain the word of God that has been sent down, they form a unity. In this sense Al-Baghdadi (who died in 1037) said: "The reading of the word of God in Arabic is the Qur'an, the reading of the Word of God in Hebrew is the Torah, and the reading of it in Syriac is the Gospel." Therefore the Qur'an calls on Muslims to declare to Jews and Christians that they – the Muslims – believe in the Torah and Gospel, as also in the revelations which have been given to the other prophets, for they are all the Word of God.' Thus it can be said that there is one religion (Islam, i.e. the peace of God), but there are three modes of faith.

So the basic meaning of Islam is not the religion founded by Muhammad which stands over against Judaism and Christianity: 'Islam means complete devotion to God, giving one's whole being to God; it means peace, salvation, and describes the state of salvation'.[18] 'Islam' means 'shalom'.[19]

Thus what may seem at first sight an exclusive claim to absoluteness is from the perspective of Islam an inclusive claim to renewal. Certainly it is a claim to final truth, but this truth is not anti-Jewish and anti-Christian, but a truth beyond Jewish and Christian truth, or primal Jewish and Christian truth, because it is genuinely divine truth. A strictly exclusive claim is advanced only against the 'unbelievers', i.e. against the polytheists who were Muhammad's main opponents in Mecca. By contrast, Jews and Christians are regarded as 'bearers of revelation' who 'possess scripture' and are constantly admonished to follow their own scriptures (5.45–48 + 69), since in the end God will also judge them according to their own scriptures (5.49). Thus the well-known principle 'There is no compulsion in religion' applies to them.[20] And Surah 29.46 states: 'Be courteous when you argue with the people of the book' – an invitation to dialogue.

I do not want to idealize. First, the description above follows the self-understanding of Islam. Christians will not be able to adopt this view of the history of revelation, nor need they. But they should know this self-understanding in order to recognize the relative recognition granted to Jews and Christians in the Qur'an.

Secondly, this was only one description of what the Qur'an says about Jews and Christians. The reality of the shaping of the relationship has not always corresponded to this definition of it. In particular the shaping of the relationship with Jews and Christians living outside the Islamic sphere was often quite hostile. Nor should it be denied that down to the present day Jews and Christians living within this sphere have had to endure massive discrimination. But it should have become clear that one can criticize such expressions of the relationship in the light of the Qur'an.

It is not the Qur'an itself which is fundamentalist; fundamentalism is bred through the application of the Qur'an by the fundamentalist Islamicists, who want to prescribe the Shari'ah (i.e. the Islamic legal order) as the absolute law of God which leads to fundamentalism. They exploit the religious renaissance for their political ends. By contrast, a look at the history of Islam (and Islam in the present) indicates how open Muslims can be to dialogue. And as we have seen, a look at the Qur'an explains why.

Hinduism and Buddhism

In Hinduism the inclusive definition of the relationship is dominant; in other words, other religions and their gods are generally related to Hinduism in a positive and inclusive way. Hindus recognize their gods as their own approach to the one divine primal ground towards which all religions strive. This leads to the 'tolerance' of Hinduism as Mahatma Gandhi describes it: 'No single religion is perfect. All religions are equally dear and valuable to their adherents. So what is needed is a living contact between the adherents of the great religions of the world and not a dispute between them, in which each community attempts in vain to demonstrate the superiority of its religion to the others.'[21]

This idea that different ways to the goal are possible does not imply the equality of religions. The plurality and difference remains, but only on the surface. Behind the manifold forms lies the one Dharma (world order, world law) as a universal religious and ethical principle. It goes beyond all religions and realizes itself in them (as in all human beings and groups) in different ways. Unity and multiplicity belong together. In this perspective, claims to absoluteness advanced by one of the religious traditions against the others can only appear as a simple limitation of the horizon of consciousness: 'It is not piety which leads to self-confident passion but a limited horizon, harshness and lack of compassion.'[22]

Underlying this is a way of thinking that knows no exclusive contrasts, because the Aristotle either-or logic is alien to it. Instead, what applies here is the 'inclusive' idea of the gradual ascent to ever higher truth, i.e. the hierarchy of lower (limited) and higher (comprehensive) truth. If two religious statements are contradictory, then according to this logic it is not that one is true and the other false. If they are both advanced by persons who are worth taking seriously and groups which are rich in tradition, they must both rather at least partially be in accord with the truth. But they are so with differing degrees of perfection. At all events, both views can be taken to a higher level. In the end there are no real contradictions, but only polarities which the wise person recognizes as complementary. Accordingly, the opposite of truth is not falsehood, but ignorance, a lack of enlightenment.

Now the Indian religions attribute precisely this wisdom to their own religion, and thus elevate this above the other religions, which have not yet advanced to such maturity. So the Indian religions in no way renounce such a claim to superiority. We shall return to this question after considering Buddhism.

Buddhism seems to be most immune to the 'absolutist' temptation. This religion has begun no religious war nor any persecution of other believers. That is true as a generalization, though Buddhists have been involved in violent disputes. As examples one need only recall the Buddhist monks who fought in Vietnam, or the oppression of the Tamil Hindus by the Buddhist Singhalese in Sri Lanka. In all these cases Buddhists offend against their own supreme command of non-violence or the inviolability of all life: not only human life but animal and plant life.

After his conversion to Buddhism, King Ashoka, who lived in India from 273 to 232 CE and ruled from 268 to 263, issued an edict which gives impressive expression to the tolerance of Buddhism in the face of the 'sects' in Indian religions.

> All religions of other men are worthy of respect for one reason or another. By respecting them one honours one's own faith and at the same time does good

to the faith of the other. If one acts otherwise, one violates one's own faith and damages that of the other, for if anyone exalts his own faith and denigrates that of another, in the service of his own confession and to glorify this, he commits a grave transgression against his own faith . . . Therefore harmony alone is good: let each listen to the other's experience of faith (*dhamma*) and follow it. For that is the wish of king Piyadassis (= Ashoka), that all religions should learn from one another.[23]

The anti-fundamentalism of Buddhist religion has found its best-known expression in the parable of the blind men feeling an elephant:[24]

A king in northern India summoned all those born blind in his city to touch the various parts of an elephant. When he then asked the blind men what an elephant looked like, each of the blind men described the 'whole' elephant in accordance with the one part that he had felt. Those who had touched the foot said, 'An elephant is like a pillar'. Those who had touched the tusk said, 'An elephant is like a ploughshare', and those who had held the hairy end of the tail in their hands said, 'An elephant is like a broom'. Now because each regarded his picture as the true one, there was a dispute among the blind men. And shouting, 'An elephant is like this, an elephant is not like that; an elephant is not like that, it is like this,' they resorted to fisticuffs.[25]

None of the blind men recognizes the elephant, but they regard their limited knowledge as complete and argue over the contradictions in their irreconcilable insights. They are blind seers. Only the king who had brought together the blind men sees the elephant, and he sees the reason for their squabble: the incompleteness of their knowledge and above all the fact that they do not concede this incompleteness, i.e. their blindness, but act as though they could see.

The parable is directed against the doctrinal egoism of the religious leaders, against the absolutizing of metaphysical doctrines, theories and speculations by the Brahmans and the ascetic miracle workers. Buddha's 'vision' is contrasted with them. He is the king who, as the one who can see, looks at what is happening and is 'amused' at it. Buddha always warned against clinging to a doctrine in blind obedience, even if it was his own. Buddha teaches a way to heal human beings of their existential sickness, the existence that is suffering. Those who follow Buddha may never be content with believing his doctrine. They must take the way themselves. Buddha's teaching is merely the occasion for this. The practice, taking the way oneself, is the goal and criterion of the teaching: 'The teaching is like a raft that one uses to get over a river (the earthly, disastrous, changing world) to the other bank (Nirvana), but which one does not take along when it has fulfilled this goal.'[26] By contrast, what does the Christian claim to absoluteness and the dispute of some Christians over 'true doctrine' look like? Buddha sees such a dispute as a sign of a lack of redemption from selfish imprisonment in oneself.

The self-limitation of Buddha's teaching results in a far-reaching recognition of other ways to salvation. 'Every way leads to the goal. Every religion is good. Do not several ways lead up Mount Fuji?'[27] This old parable told all over Japan alludes to the different pilgrim ways leading to the summit of the holy mountain Fuji-san.

There are many other Indian and Buddhist parables about the origin, nature or aim of the religions, about their common basis despite the difference in their form. To express the ultimate unity in plurality – the sameness in the difference – the religions are compared with the different reflections of the one moon on the waters of the earth;[28] with the different coloured refractions of the one light in a prism;[29] with the different fingers of a hand;[30] different panes of glass or windows through which the one sun shines; different rivers (or canals) in which the same water flows from the same source or which issue in the same ocean; with the colours of a rainbow, the branches of a tree or the spokes of a wheel, which all end up at the hub. The motif in this series of images is always the same: the religions are many, and they are different; the gods called on by them are different and the faces of the gods presented by them are different, but what inspires the religons, what the names denote and what the faces point to, is one and the same.

That the one divine primal ground has different names, and the difference in religions corresponds to the difference in languages, is also a motif in Ramakrishna's best-known parable. He tells of a reservoir to which different stairways lead: 'From one the Hindus draw water in jars and call it "jal"; from another Muslims draw water in leather skins and call it "pani"; from a third Christians draw water and call it "water". Can we think that the water is not "jal", but only "pani" or "water"? How ridiculous! The substance is one, but it has different names, and each seeks the same substance.'[31]

Anyone who absolutizes particular names misses the one substance which underlies all the names. A claim to sole and exclusive
validity has no genuine place in religions of Indian origin;[32] it is
regarded as backward and provincial.

But on the other hand that does not mean that in affirming the
unity of the ground of transcendence the sages of these religions
want to claim that all religions are the same. The capacity of one's
religion for integration, its tolerance and the universality of its
horizon are regarded as signs of religious maturity and in this way
form a claim to superiority. This is what the narrator of the elephant
parable is also doing in giving only the king (= Buddha) the capacity
of sight. This is also a kind of claim to absolutes, albeit not a sharply
exclusive one but an inclusive one. From this standpoint the other
religions do not appear as errors but as by-ways, which perhaps point
in the right direction, but are still (in different senses) a long way
from their goal.

The following saying of the Buddha, quoted by Phra Khantipalo,
shows that this inclusive claim to superiority can even be intensified
to become a claim to sole validity. Here the Buddha unequivocally
expresses the uniqueness of his own doctrine: 'Of all the ways the
Eightfold Path is the best; of all the truths the Four Noble Truths are
the best . . . that is the only way, there is no other way of reaching
purity of insight.'[33]

The superiority of one's own religion and the different degrees of
inferiority in other religions are expressed in the form of step-
ladders. Thus the Shingon sect of Japanese Mahayana Buddhism
recognizes ten steps in religion; the second is occupied by Confucia-
nism; the third by Taoism and Brahmanism; the fourth and fifth are
assigned to the sects of Hinayana Buddhism; the sixth to the ninth to
the sects of Mahayana Buddhism; while the tenth – as might be
expected – is reserved for the Shingon sect itself. Christianity must
be content with the second step.[34]

Such ten-step ladders make it possible to 'neutralize' rival religions by the
order in which they are put. They can be found in many religions, including
Islam and Christianity. Thus on the bottom step of an Islamic scheme there
are the idolaters and unbelievers, on the eighth step the Jews, on the ninth the
Christians, and on the top step the Muslims. The Japanese Christian
Toyohiko Kagawa takes up the Japanese parable of climbing Fuji-san

mentioned above, but characteristically turns it round. He grants that all the religions are on the way to the summit, but some of them 'already stop at the sixth resting place . . . some at the fourth, and some get tired and rest before they have even passed the first resting place . . . Buddhism may bring us to the ninth resting place, but because it rests there, I do not choose Buddhism, because I want to get to the top.'[35]

Broken absoluteness

This journey through the individual so-called mystical and prophetic religions leads to the following conclusions.

It would be short-sighted and dangerous to call a religion as a whole, far less all prophetic religions together, 'absolutist', and by contrast to call the mystical religions 'dialogical'. Hans-Jochen Margull's remark that 'each religion understands itself as unique, final, universal, and thus essentially complete and perfect'[36] applies at least to the great world religions (if not to each religion in the same way, least of all in the case of Judaism). The tendency in religions of Indian origin is for this 'claim to absoluteness' to appear in an inclusive form and in the Abrahamic religions in an exclusive form. However, it does not follow that those religions with an inclusive attitude towards other religions are open to dialogue: inclusivism can go with arrogant tendencies to commandeering, which can be as hostile to dialogue as exclusive claims to sole validity.

The sweeping verdict that prophetic religions are necessarily bound up with the claim to exclusiveness does not apply to any of them, either to Christianity or to Islam or – perhaps least of all – to Judaism. Certainly each of these three religions has its absolute basis of faith which it will not surrender (because this foundation provides its identity): Jews have their conviction of the election of Israel as the people of God who brought them up out of Egypt and promised them the Holy Land; Christians have the doctrine of Christ as the only Son of God in whom alone God's salvation is given to us; and Muslims have the view that the Qur'an is the ultimate word of God, because it is verbally inspired, unfalsified and thus infallible. But on the other hand these religions always have approaches which prevent absolute claims being made for the religion, i.e. for the manifestation of the revelation. It was the prophetic protest in particular which castigated the prophetic religions when they made themselves absolute; the prophets saw this as one of the fundamental sins, if not *the* sin: proud human self-righteousness before God. Just as Islam – the primal revelation of divine salvation – relativizes Islamic religion, so Christ relativizes the Christian religion and 'the law and the prophets' relativize the Jewish religion.

Paul Tillich (1886–1965) sees this prophetic protest against religious self-absolutizing as a 'Protestant principle' at work in all religions.[37] For all religions are involved in the tension between formation and protest: the primal ground of all being, God himself, creates endless manifestations of himself in the religions; he enters into human beings, human words, holy scriptures, religious rites, laws and institutions. Here it comes about time and again that these 'figures of grace' are divinized, i.e. that the finite is elevated to the level of the infinite; the human to Christ; the verbal expression to the Bible; the material to the sacrament; the institutional to the church.[38] The truth underlying religion is put in a sacral prison; religion gets lost in the elements by which it is described. The prophetic protest is directed against such reifications of God. No dogma, no confession, no holy scripture, no doctrine, no religious authority can and may claim the holiness of God for itself. Though the mixture of form and protest within the individual prophetic (and mystical) religions may be very different, the 'Protestant principle' is nowhere without effect.[39] And particularly in the roots of the prophetic religions an element of self-criticism has been engraved which forbids all religious triumphalism and any claim to absoluteness which a religion makes for itself.

16

A Very Different Way: Christianity without a Claim to Absoluteness

The move towards dialogue

Within only a few decades the Christian view of other religions has undergone an epoch-making change in the ecumenical movement. Whereas the 1910 World Missionary Conference in Edinburgh was still about helping Christianity towards a final victory over the religions, today there are more and more calls for an equal partnership between the religions. In Edinburgh, John R. Mott, the leader of the World Missionary Conference, called for the 'Evangelization of the World in this Generation'. The assembly appealed to the Christian churches: 'It is a spiritual demand that we cannot avoid that the whole of life and everything which radiates from the nations should be Christianized, so that the whole influence, including trade and politics, of the West on the East and the stronger nations on the weaker should strengthen and not weaken the missionary message.'[1] One detects how near this sense of mission is to the spirit of Eurocentric imperialism and colonialism which was aware of a vocation to contribute not only Christianity, but also Western civilization towards the education of a world that was underdeveloped in both cultural and religious terms.

With that I would contrast the call to 'Reconciliation with Those of Other Religions' which was approved by the General Assembly of the World Council of Churches in Canberra in 1991:[2] 'The Bible bears witness to God as the ruler over all nations and peoples, whose love and concern is extended to all of humankind. In the covenant with Noah we see a covenant of God with all creation. We recall the covenant which God made with Abraham and Israel. In the history of this covenant we are promised that we will recognize God through Jesus Christ. We are also aware that others bear witness to having experienced God in another way. We are witnesses to the truth that salvation is in Jesus Christ, and we are also open to the witness of others who encounter the truth differently.' What is called for is a 'culture of dialogue' as a way of reconciliation, a dialogue which overcomes ignorance and intolerance.

A recognition of the non-Christian religions which goes still further was expressed by those who participated in a consultation which took place at the WCC sub-division 'Dialogue with People of Living Religions' in Baar, Switzerland (9–15 January 1990).[3] There the plurality of religions is understood as the 'result of the many ways in which God has communicated himself to peoples and nations' [231]. There, too, believers have 'found redemption, totality, illumination, divine guidance, rest and liberation' [231]. God's redeeming mystery 'has been communicated and expressed in many different ways which unfold as God's plan towards its fulfilment. There may be ways which we do not know for those outside the flock (John 10.6) if they live faithfully and truly in their particular circumstances and within the framework of the religious traditions which guide and inspire them' [233].

Certainly these three highlights – Edinburgh, Canberra and Baar – are not a complete description of the development of the Christian attitude towards the non-Christian religions, but they do indicate an important tendency. Nor should we forget that as early as 1894 there was a World Parliament of Religions in Chicago at which the Hindu missionary Vivekananda appealed for reconciliation between the religions; that the 'World Congress for Free Christianity and Religious Progress' took place in Berlin in 1910;[4] and that in 1921 Rudolf Otto founded the 'Religious Alliance of Mankind': this is the other side to the growth of fundamentalism in the present that I have already described.[5]

Nevertheless, we must speak of a change, of a paradigm shift, in the relationship of Christianity to the religions: the 'one-way street' has become open to two-way traffic;[6] the one-sided monologues have been supplemented (but not replaced!) with a readiness to listen and understand. For Catholicism this change coincides with the Second Vatican Council,[7] and for the Protestant branch of Christianity it can be dated to 1967. In that year delegates of the WCC met at Kandy in Sri Lanka, and there declared: 'It is being recognized throughout the world that people of different religions should encounter one another not in dispute, but in friendship. As Christians we confess that in the past we have been lacking in both love and understanding. It is now our honest wish to enter into dialogue with those of other faiths.'[8] At the 1971 session of the WCC Central Committee in Addis Ababa the division on 'Dialogue with People of Other Religions and Ideologies' was founded, and thus interreligious dialogue was institutionalized. A series of bilateral and multilateral consultations between Christians and representatives of other religions followed.[9] But these dialogues threw up more and more theological questions which called for clarification. What theological judgment is to be passed on the religions? Is God at work in them, and if so, how? Is there authentic worship of God within them, so that one could even find forms for shared worship with them? and so on.[10]

How are we to explain the shift from monologue to dialogue over recent decades? I shall now go on to describe changes in the external situation and a change in the cultural framework which seem to me to be responsible for this shift. Then I want to present some theological ideas which show that by virtue of its deepest basis Christian faith is orientated on dialogue, so that it can be said that the shift towards dialogue is not a fashionable adaptation to the spirit of the age, but an expression of true Christianity. Hence my plea for a Christianity without claims to absoluteness.

A changed situation

Here is a brief, thumbnail sketch.

The experience of the two World Wars and the end of European colonial imperialism dealt a healthy blow to any sense of superiority in Western Christianity. The political and economic focus shifted to great powers outside Europe. Asia and Africa emerged as independent 'cultural great powers'. In this way their religions also came increasingly into the perspective of Western Christianity.

Whereas with increasing secularization the Christian religion lost more and more social significance in the Western world, other world religions (like Hinduism and Islam) underwent a renaissance. With growing self-awareness they began to carry on missions in the heartlands of contemporary Christianity.

One factor contributing towards the new openness to dialogue which should not be underestimated is the assimilation of guilt. Anyone aware of the spiritual support that the churches gave to colonialism, anyone familiar with the war sermons of the First World War, anyone lamenting the silence of too many Christians in the face of the persecution of the Jews under National Socialism will be mistrustful of Christian absolutism and particularism.

The world has become a global village. As a result of the communication network of the mass media throughout the world and also the almost unlimited possibilities for travel, encounter with other cultures and religions is open to anyone who is interested in it. And quite a few people return home deeply impressed with such encounters. 'A survey of the history of religion first of all arouses in a sensitive religious disposition a feeling of reverence, awe and wonderment at the countless forms in which human beings seek and ask after the eternal God and in which God discloses himself to the longing and loving heart . . . In view of all the holiness and greatness disclosed by the non-Christian religions, the view of the "orthodox", that "before the introduction of Christianity all the peoples of the earth were nothing but outcasts, forsaken and forgotten by the Father in heaven, without knowledge of God and without hope of heaven", collapses.'[11]

In addition there is an awareness of the global dimension of the tasks which humanity faces (this has been discussed in Chapter 5). That the human race for the first time in history has the possibility of destroying itself along with the whole planet earth – to mention just one of the problems – calls for a counter-reaction which equally involves all of humankind. And only joint efforts by as many as possible can get us further in the fight for justice, peace and the preservation of creation. Confessionalism, religious provincialism and quarrelling over the right doctrine of salvation are obstacles along this way. Where Christianity recognizes that it is one religion alongside others in a non-Christian world, yet does not hold back from contributing the inestimable riches of its tradition to a partnership of religions, it can make an important contribution towards removing such obstacles. I have referred earlier to the need for constant peacemaking in multi-religious societies and inter-religious areas.

The changed understanding of truth

A second stimulus towards openness to encounter in religious dialogue lies in a spiritual 'paradigm shift' which has affected and fundamentally changed all spheres of intellectual life in European and American culture. Our notion of 'truth' has undergone a process of de-absolutizing and de-objectifying.

Leonard Swidler sums up this change in six points:[12] 1. All truth now holds only in relation to the historical context in which it was produced, i.e. it is historically conditioned and thus involved in constant change. 2. In addition to this contextual conditioning there is the orientation of actions, i.e. the intention behind a practical action. 3. Truth is related to a standpoint; i.e., the cultural milieu in which the speaker and hearer of a communication of truth live, the class they belong to and their sex have an influence on the truth communicated. 4. Truth is bound up with language and thus limited to its frontiers; in other words, it always expresses a partial, selective, perspectivistic view of reality. 5. Truth is subject to interpretation, i.e. all experience relates back to a horizon of understanding, to the preunderstanding of the person experiencing it. The knower is involved in the knowledge since he or she knows in his or her way (as Thomas Aquinas recognized[13]). There can be no such thing as purely objective, absolute knowledge, detached from the knowing subject. 6. Truth is dialogical, i.e. knowledge is achieved not in the mode of a one-sided acceptance of givens but reciprocally in dialogue with reality following the model of question and answer.

If we take these six tendencies together – and it is certainly impossible to make a sharp distinction between them – we can say that 'truth' no longer means absolute, i.e. detached, isolated, unconditional statements about reality. It is relational, and stands in relation to a network which is conditioned by many factors. But above all it is related to the one who receives it and expresses it; it is and remains tied to this person's point of view, perspective and language. There can no longer be any question of absoluteness in the sense of something that transcends time and culture, is independent of world-view and set apart from history.

Paul Knitter expresses this shift when he says that according to the new mode truth is no longer defined by its capacity to exclude or absorb other truths but, conversely, by its capacity to relate positively to other truth claims and through this exchange to arrive at mutual growth. Relationality, mutuality and openness to dialogue have become almost the criteria for truth (in place of exclusiveness).[14] Raimondo Panikkar goes in the same direction when he writes: 'Truth cannot be reduced either to unity or to plurality. It is always relationship, and therefore allows neither singularity or plurality.'[15]

Such relationality is not synonymous with relativity or even with a relativism of all truths, values and foundations of faith. It does not lead to the groundless scepticism of a 'universal "perhaps" which regards everything as possible because nothing is binding'.[16] One can also see the unlimited and universal from a limited standpoint and in a particular perspective.

The need for stability in the certainty of faith is quite compatible with a de-objectivized conception of the truth. Christians need in no way give up the certainty of their faith, but must simply become aware that they 'see' with the eyes of believers.

At this point I want to introduce a distinction which has become important for me in interpreting the claim to absoluteness: H. Richard Niebuhr (1894–1962) distinguishes between 'internal' and 'external' history, between the personal history that we see from our faith and the actual history that an uninvolved observer (say a historian) describes.[17] The two perspectives are not mutually exclusive; the personal perspective sees more than just a sequence of events. It takes part in the events, 'sees' them in a particular sense, sees them 'as'. But because the personal view is tied up with the one who has it and remains so, it cannot be universally valid; it is always only individual (which does not mean subjectivistic or solipsistic). Its time is not linear chronological time, for which past is past and future is future. It is qualitative time, for which past events and future expectations are present and significant. We are not in it, but it is in us.

When Christians speak of revelation in history, as I shall do in the next section, it is 'their' history of which they speak: history viewed with the eyes of faith, which is constitutive of their faith community. An 'event' like the resurrection of Christ plays a central role in it, whereas this event is insignificant for a historian. This inner history of Christians cannot simply be described; it has to be made present in narrative, confessed; one has to put oneself into it in order to take part in it.

That does not open the door wide to the suspicion of projection, which seeks to reduce God's action to inner history and to pretend that it is the product of the Christian imagination. God acts in outward history, but discloses this action only to those who allow him to open their eyes to it.

A religious 'positivism of facts' which I described in Chapter 3 identifies the inner with the outer history and thus misunderstands the nature of God's revelation. By contrast, the relational understanding of truth described above not only lies nearer to the thought of many of our contemporaries than the Greek (Platonic) notion of a trans-historical, unchangeable and eternally valid truth, but also corresponds better to the biblical view of truth.

For in the Bible truth in no way means the cognitive content of an assertion, but an attestation of personal reliability, steadfastness and faithfulness. The truth of God is not a doctrine which seeks to be regarded as true; it is a spiritual power which is to be *done* (John 3.21). So 'truth' means far more than the validity of Christian doctrines and confessions; it is about the right way of life, about true participation in the truth of God. In this 'practical' sense truth is synonymous with 'truthfulness' as the true, authentic encounter with God.

M. von Brück has investigated the lingustic roots of the concept of truth. It emerges from his work that in German and English, too, the original meaning of truth focusses not so much on knowledge as on faithfulness and reliability: the German word *Wahrheit* is derived from the Old High German *war* or *wara*, and that is an oath of loyalty. *Giwari* in Old High German is then 'bound in loyalty', certain and sure through loyalty. The English word 'truth' comes from the Old English *triewo* or *treowo* (a loyal promise), and in its derivative 'truthfulness' still means fidelity and reliability, like the German word *Wahrhaftigkeit*.[18]

That brings us to the third stimulus for Christian openness to dialogue. Important impulses in this direction stem from the heart of Christian faith itself. First of all there is quite simply the ethical imperative to solidarity, i.e. the recollection that co-operation in forming a relationship, fellowship and dialogue are more in keeping with the spirit of the gospel than an aggressive confrontation.[19] But there are yet other fundamental theological insights which could form the basis for a dialogical encounter of religions. We now turn to those. Here it will prove that the Christian claim to absoluteness cannot be grounded in a reference to God's revelation, as has constantly happened.

Revelation as event

There are two opposed themes in the biblical tradition, both of which prohibit the grounding of religious claims to absoluteness on God's revelation: 1. God opens himself, 'reveals' himself, enters into concrete situations; and 2. God withdraws, remains hidden and preserves his mystery.

1. According to the biblical understanding, revelation has the character of event; it is an event which is not under our control. It is not the communication of intellectual truths which exclude other truths; it is not an extension of the knowledge of the world to a knowledge of things beyond the world. Revelation essentially means the history on which God goes, along with human beings: the history of the fellowship of God with humankind.

So the truth of God is *not* unhistorical – therein lies the decisive difference from the Greek understanding of truth. It has become a part of the human world and has thus exposed itself to relativity, i.e. to social and cultural influences, expressed in different ways in space and time. It is not universal and unchangeable, but historical and concrete, related to places and thus dynamic. This follows not least from the heart of the Christian knowledge of God: from belief in the incarnation of God. We shall return to that.

The history of God with humankind handed down in the Bible has made God known as a God of the way, who goes along with his wandering people and speaks to a particular context in concrete terms, related to the situation. So his truth does not take place absolutely, i.e. detached from the historical reality of human beings, but in relation to specific circumstances. It is the one critical-creative relationship.

The authors of the biblical writings attest that God's plan with the world exists from eternity and does not change. But the revelations of this plan are given concretely in situations and are therefore never comprehensive and universally valid, nor can they be transferred directly from one situation to another. God's revelation, which people are so fond of using to justify Christian claims to absoluteness, is not something absolute, not something static, not something given once and for all, but a becoming, a becoming ever new; it is not a given, but God's power in the world which builds up and destroys. In the same way 'God is never merely the invisible ground of present reality, but the free, creative source of the ever new and unforeseen'.[20]

That the truth of God becomes part of the human world and is thus incarnated in the culture of a particular time does not mean that this truth loses its validity by thus entering into the concrete world in which people live. On the contrary, precisely in its self-emptying it proves its effectiveness, guarantees it and preserves it. And it does so not by fending off assertions to the contrary but by its power to heal the sick, to break through conventions hostile to humanity and to liberate men and women from the power of death in the midst of life. It cannot be contained in statements and doctrines, but occurs only where it takes place: not in the orthodoxy of the letter but in that spirit which calls for solidarity with the least of the brethren and makes this possible. And so one cannot 'have' it, but only live in it.[21] It is not to be assserted but to be done. For it is not dogma but the creative and healing power of God, i.e. that which puts together what has been separated.

Where a Christian claim to absoluteness is made, where the creative dynamic presence of God is petrified so that it becomes a truth which is thus and not otherwise, timeless and universally valid, truth preserves its revolutionary force precisely by bursting such bonds.

On this basis we can and must criticize the supposed 'loyalty' to the Bible of Christian fundamentalists. In presenting the truth of God as information about supernatural facts and events which go from the sender to the recipient by revelation, they promote naive everyday consciousness to be the criterion of biblical exegesis. In so doing they have imposed their need for direct access to a direct truth of God removed from all cultural influences on the autonomy of this truth which is beyond human control. The text of the Bible is no longer taken seriously as something strange because it stands over against us, which can also be the cause of a radical shaking of our own certainty of faith – a disturbing fact, not for others, supposed to be unbelievers, but in particular for the pious, the Pharisees and scribes of all times. Where one's own thought and faith are read into the text of the Bible, to be read out of it again, the biblical tradition is devalued, so that it merely confirms what the exegetes had always thought and known. If their understanding of the Bible seems uncomplicated, it is only because it is not really a concern for authentic understanding.

The biblical texts are not factual accounts, but existential reports which make God's activity present; they are not simply reports about the reality of God and the world, but reports about a life drawing on the sources of God's living power. They do not communicate any new knowledge about God and the world but a new perspective – a view of the world through God's eyes. In this sense, what we have is not information but testimony.

The certainty of faith is never knowledge of the facts of salvation which could be brought under our control in statements and dogmas capable of being objectified. It is trust in a relationship, a relationship with God. So it can and must be said that 'Christians do not have certainty and certainly do not have certainties. The plural is always suspicious. Rather, they become certain through being involved in God's history, which is made concrete in Jesus Christ.'[22]

God's entry into concrete historical situations is the first theme which prevents us from making an unhistorical claim to absoluteness. Now let us turn to the second:

2. That God's truth enters into history does not mean that it is exhausted in history. God's infinite and unfathomable mystery remains sovereign over all solidified forms of God's revelation: it transcends them and relativizes them. It remains the absolute, the '*Deus semper maior*' (the God who is always greater) 'who dwells in light inaccessible' (I Tim.6.16).

'The reality of God remains an inexpressible and inexhaustible mystery beyond our experience; it has not been completely recognized by any religion, and indeed this is impossible in principle. God preserves the mystery of his name; at best we can see only his "back", and must be content with fragmentary knowledge.'[23]

Anyone who claims that the final and universal revelation of God lies in the Christian message forgets that even this message will be taken up into God at the end of time (I Cor.15.28). Only at the end of time will God's complete and full truth be manifest. The New Testament preserves the tension between the 'now already', what God has done in Jesus Christ, and the 'not yet', the final completion which is yet to come. Christ is not only the one who has come but also the one who is to come. Time and again he points out that the final redemption will take place only when the Son of Man comes, at the end of time. His resurrection is only an anticipation of this: it gives us hope for this redemption. But as long as time has not yet come to an end, unredeemed existence continues. Anyone in this situation who makes the claim already now to possess the final truth to its full extent relaxes the tension between the 'already' and the 'not yet' by putting excessive emphasis on the former. So it is not just any testimony to the message of Christ, but this message itself which stands under an 'eschatological proviso'.

The truth of the message is thus also 'open in a forward direction'. Jesus points beyond himself to the coming Son of Man, and he points to God (John 12.44),[24] in whose name he has come as Christ (John 5.43). He does not seek his own honour (John 8.50) but sacrifices 'everything in him and from him which could bring people to him as an "overwhelming personality"'.[25] The way in which Jesus points beyond himself is the counterbalance to the christocentrism in John which was described in Chapter 8 above.

God's full truth is only disclosed in the light of the goal of history. It is not something fixed once and for all which always only needs to be proclaimed afresh; its character is one of becoming; it is on the way to an ever greater consummation in a dynamic process. In this development it combines the particular individual truths in an ever greater unity by deepening the relationship between them until they come together in the eschatological goal of the 'all in all' (I Cor.15.28). However, to any particular present it always remains as what is ever before it, pointing towards the future and therefore the ground of all being which is only to be striven for, and which can never wholly be grasped and possessed.[26]

Truth-claims and dialogue

'Let every one be fully convinced in his own mind' (Rom.14.5).

Where we speak of a cosmic universality of our Creator God we must also concede that this God is at work bringing salvation throughout the world. And where we speak of an all-embracing redemption through Jesus Christ, we cannot make it dependent on a particular state of knowledge. Finally, where we speak of a spirit of God which blows where it wills, over all boundaries of nation, culture and religion, we must refrain from any petty attempt to exclude others from this truth.

Now if God works where he does work, concretely in situations without being exhausted in them, the truth which God makes event cannot be monolithic. God's truth, which is certainly one 'in itself', can only present itself in the plurality of particular views of the truth. And if this plurality is unavoidable and cannot be given up within history, the recognition of other forms of faith and dialogue with them is the inescapable consequence.

Dialogue here means something quite different from a 'negotiation', the aim of which is to reach agreement over convictions of faith. That is a completely absurd notion. The necessary plurality of these convictions cannot be done away with; that would be absolutist, and demonstrate an imperialism of salvation. Dialogue is not a method of carrying on a conversation, nor is it a philosophical discussion; it is a basic attitude, a disposition towards those of other faiths: 'dialogue is a life-style related to the neighbour',[27] moreover 'an attitude brought about by Christ'.[28] It is not the aim of encounter in dialogue to arrive at a consensus over the contents of faith but (a) to correct false ideas, (b) to improve interpersonal relationships, (c) to bring liberation from anxiety, (d) to deepen one's own faith, and (e) to lead down the way to unity.[29]

'To lead down the way to unity' does not mean striving for a single world religion. Historically, such an effort has always been the expression of a political, cultural and religious totalitarianism which would seek to incorporate the religions in one guiding religion.[30]

'Unity' does not mean having one form, being one. 'Unity' does not mean unification of convictions in an innocuous striving for harmony, but giving them profile in a concern for mutual understanding; it is not uniformity, but communion in an abiding difference. The forms of faith should not be fused, nor should each neutralize the other. Each of the partners continues on its way and may even press forward along it. But a fundamental mutual acceptance of the different ways remains. It does not have its foundation primarily in enlightened tolerance but in the presupposition that the other's way also comes from God and leads to God. The other is recognized as a witness to the divine. That being so, a relationship of parity prevails between the partners: not equality but equal rights.

Dialogue is practice in adopting each other's perspective, practice in the art of seeing with the eyes of the other. And that also means practice in the art of seeing oneself with the eyes of the other.[31] Here one's own view cannot remain unchanged. Therefore dialogue involves the constant conversion of the partner. Where the necessary readiness to learn and therefore always to allow oneself to be changed is lacking on one side or the other, dialogue cannot succeed. So it has to be said that:

1. The claim to absoluteness is incompatible with dialogue. Where one side encounters the other in the attitude of one who has a monopoly of the truth, a dialogue cannot be a real encounter in mutual respect. No committed and interested grappling with the truth can take place, but only the propagation of one's own position, that claims all truth for itself and therefore is ultimately uninterested in the faith of the other. One's own faith is directly opposed to the other with a feeling that the other's faith is utterly insignificant for one's own.

To those claiming a monopoly of the truth it must be objected that no one can ever claim for themselves the truth of God which is always particular, never completely within our grasp and always open to the future. But the firm conviction of being 'in' the truth, of being near to it and on the way which leads closer and closer to this truth that transcends all particular human truth and thus also all particular religious truth – this awareness is the ground of the certainty of the Christian's faith as it is the ground of the faith of all believers. A claim to truth understood in this way need be neither exclusive nor inclusive; without forfeiting its binding nature, it can leave room for other occurrences of the truth, which for its part is more than the sum of all its events. So we can say:

2. Not only are dialogue and the claim to truth incompatible, but the one requires the other. Dialogue needs participants who do not give up their particular claims to the truth – if they did, what would there be to talk about? Anyone to whom the conviction of faith is serious and important cannot simply mean to engage in insignificant small talk. And conversely, those who lay claim to the truth need dialogue, mutual enrichment and deepening if they are not to withdraw smugly into their own possession of truth but reach out to the truth of the God who is always greater.

Although it is those who are convinced who encounter one another in dialogue, not those who are still seeking, ideally dialogue can become the place where God is known: knowledge through understanding the other; understanding the other by coming to an understanding with the other. Understanding the other not only deepens our understanding of ourselves, but also deepens our understanding of God who has not left the other – who like us is in the image of God – without witness.

But this ideal can only come about if Christians do not feel that they have to give up their Christian identity at the gateway to inter-religious dialogue in order permanently to be able to give themselves to others in *their* religious identity. Such a dialogue would not be a dialogue at all, but again only a boring monologue. Christian dialogue partners should not allow themselves to be 'tossed to and fro and carried about with every wind of doctrine' (Eph.4.14); they should not accept everything uncritically and thus expose their own perspective to a universalistic dilution. Dialogue requires each side to give a full and uncurtailed account of its own way of believing. And that presupposes that the different convictions are expressed authentically with their unconditional truth-claims. The fact that dialogue is concerned with whole schemes of life, world-views and orientations for action which are existentially fundamental for those who hold them gives it its radical tension and often – if this tension is really sustained – makes it a real test.

Where I cannot perceive the conviction of the other with a benevolent and detached interest because it puts me and my conviction overwhelmingly in question, where I must respond to the other with an uncompromising 'no' because I cannot and am no longer willing to understand this other whose thought and action I find abhorrent, the fundamental insight is disclosed that dialogue is also and not least a matter of suffering through the other (which is the meaning of 'tolerance' in the real sense of the word).

This suffering through the other also includes the experience of a refusal to engage in dialogue, the bitter experience that the one with whom I would like to enter into dialogue rejects this desire or enters into it only with superficial politeness. Dialogue is possible only when the partners are ready for it. Where readiness for an encounter in dialogue is lacking – and it is lacking in many adherents of all religions – there will be no dialogue. But whether this readiness is lacking and whether it cannot be aroused will only emerge where a serious attempt is made to engage in dialogue.

Where, by contrast, an encounter in dialogue is successful, neither of the partners should be afraid to show the special character of their faith with all its peculiarities. They should not be afraid that this will be too much for their dialogue partner. Christians can describe this special character with relaxed sovereignty, without any urgency. For them, this relaxed feeling arises from the awareness that they are not the ones who have to lead the others into the truth, but rather that it is the Spirit of God who leads them and others into all truth. So openness to dialogue presupposes a quiet trust in one's own certainty of the truth which on the other hand is aware of the ultimate relativity of all religious truth. Only those who rest in their own truth like this can allow themselves completely to empty themselves in order to understand others at their deepest foundations. Where uncertainty in faith, anxiety about one's own trust, a lack of trust in the truth of God which is always ahead of us and in the end transcends all human confessions of faith prevails, the result is the fortress mentality of the narrow-minded zealots for the faith who fear dialogue as a betrayal of the (their) truth and obsessively withdraw to their own religious foundations.

Such sovereignty does not exclude a dispute over the truth. I will object to much that I encounter in the religions, above all in the so-called new religious movements. This is not only because it is contrary to the message of Christ but first of all because it does not meet the criteria mentioned above for proving it in life.

Nor does such sovereignty exclude the possibility that Christians may feel compelled to drop the basic attitude of dialogue and oppose intolerance with intolerance: where – as we saw in Chapter 6 – a clear veto is called for against powers which are hostile to humanity and thus to God, where a totalitarian, 'absolutist' opponent who violates basic human rights (including the right to freedom to practise one's religion) compels total opposition. This is an unavoidable heightening of tension which can and must be relaxed again when the threat has been averted. It may not become consolidated into a habit, i.e. a basic attitude.

Dialogue as a basic attitude means finding a middle way between fanaticism about the truth and forgetfulness of the truth, between rigid 'absolutism' and rampant 'pluralism'. The necessary condition for inter-religious dialogue is not a renunciation of truth-claims; without that the dialogue would lose its seriousness. Nor is the goal of dialogue to decide between rival claims or even find a consensus. The only possible condition for dialogue is an observance of the basic ethical law of mutuality, i.e. of reciprocal recognition. According to this basic law, the other is accorded the right to his or her claim to the truth; the other is supposed to be capable of the truth and faithful to the truth along his or her religious way. The question that the other puts to one's own faith is taken seriously; one's own truth-claim must demonstrate its viability in the face of this question and vice versa. It is this that gives the discussion its deep significance.

The account so far has left aside the question of power; my presupposition has always been an encounter of partners who in principle are of equal strength. But in reality there is often a difference in the power of those involved in an encounter. This difference always begins with the choice of the place of the dialogue and the language in which it is held; those who enter into dialogue on their own ground and in their own language are far 'stronger' than those who have to use a foreign language in an alien place. In addition there is the question of the degree of theological competence – a priest with an academic training has different possibilities of expression from an itinerant Buddhist ascetic. And not least there are many differences relating to economic and ethnic backgrounds, class and gender, which are or could be power factors in the dialogue. Where no account is taken of these differences in power – in their different manifestations – the demand for equal rights for the partners can only mean that more room should be given to the weaker than to the stronger. Thus Paul Knitter has constantly put forward the demand that the underprivileged should be given a privileged position in dialogue.[32]

In these last considerations it has already become clear that alongside the 'spiritual' presuppositions of dialogue there are also quite practical conditions that must be fulfilled. There must be 'room' – in the literal as well as in the metaphorical sense – for the encounter. Furthermore, there must also be space where the other faith community can assemble in order to be together and live out its faith. However, such spaces are not freely available. Persons and institutions have the power to open them up or to close them off. Here it very soon becomes evident that dialogue does not take place in the sub-tropical climate of freedom from domination. As I already said in Chapter 3, making space for others is already part of the attitude of dialogue. Specifically, that can mean supporting the introduction of Muslim religious instruction in schools, or celebrating Muslim festivals alongside Christian ones in kindergarten. Or it can mean helping to create possibilities of encounter with adherents of other religions in church communities.[33] Those who control such spaces determine whether or not encounters in dialogue come about.

Making space for the faith of others in one's own life and thought must also mean making space for them in Christian theology. Thus not only the working out of a 'theology of religions' is called for, but also the development of theology against the experiential background of the inter-religious event of encounter. Here it is possible to sketch out what that could mean only in broad outline.

Given this understanding of the encounter of religions in dialogue, is mission still possible? There can and must be mission; no longer, however, as a one-sided evangelization with the aim of converting but as part of involvement in God's mission. *God* is the missionary. 'Mission is the ongoing action of God through the Spirit in order to heal the broken creation, to overcome the splintering of humanity and to bridge the gulf between human beings, nature and God.'[34] It is the task of Christians to 'let your light so shine before men, that they may see your good works and give glory to your Father who is in heaven' (Matt.5.16). We are to help in the work of God's Spirit as it has manifested itself in Christ – in words, but above all in our behaviour. Thus testimony to Christ 'in the Spirit and in power' (I Cor.2.4) is hindered rather than helped by claims about the absoluteness of our own faith. Mission is always a new conversion to God – conversion not only of the others but also and not least of those who say 'Lord, Lord' (Matt.7.21).

Testing the spirits

> 'No one should . . . have any views on any other aspect of interreligious questions until he or she has a friend among them' (W. Cantwell Smith)

The question of mission leads us even deeper into the description of what happens in dialogue. For here it becomes clear that the encounter in dialogue consists not only in an empathetic sensitivity to the view of the other but also in the confessional presentation and defence of one's own conviction. Whereas the empathetic attitude leads us to put ourselves in the perspective of the other in order to be able to experience it from within, the confessional attitude allows us to understand the other 'from outside', in the light of Christian categories. An empathetic orientation requires us to see others and their reality with their eyes, and requires others to attempt to see us and our reality with our eyes. The confessional attitude, however, involves our seeing others and their reality with our eyes, just as it requires them to see us and our reality with their eyes.[35] This reciprocal interplay of standing in one's own perspective and departing from it, of insisting and transcending, of a confessional and an empathetic attitude, make up true dialogue. Where it is dissolved by one side or the other, the dialogical encounter dies.[36]

Mutual testing of forms of faith is possible and necessary in the polarity of these two directions. Testing here does not mean judging (that would be the consequence of an absolutized confessional attitude),[37] but it does not mean allowing everything either (that would be the consequence of an absolutized empathetic attitude). It means accepting the strangeness of the other without abandoning the special character of one's own faith.

A criterion is needed for mutual critical testing of forms of faith. And for those concerned, this criterion is provided by the basic values of their own particular traditions. There is no third element which transcends both and to which both could refer. So there must also be agreement on criteria in dialogue. Overlaps will be noted, but these never become identity.[38]

Hans Küng has identified a hierarchy of three criteria. He proceeds 'inwardly as it were in the form of a spiral in three movements: from the universally ethical to the universally religious, and only from there to the specifically Christian'.[39] He first mentions the *humanum* as a universal ethical criterion. What violates the human dignity and human life cannot be true and good before God. The universal religious criterion runs: a religion is true and good 'if and in so far as it remains true to its own origin or canon, to its authentic "nature", its normative scripture or figures and constantly refers to it'.[40] And 'according to the specifically Christian criterion a religion is true and good if and in so far as it shows the Spirit of Jesus in its theory and praxis'.[41]

I would like to set alongside (not over against) Küng's criteria a threefold standard for testing individual faith (not religion, but the life of faith). This criterion has certainly grown up on Christian soil, but it can also be used beyond it. It investigates the forms of faith (both Christian and non-Christian) by the way in which they are put into practice in actual life. What are the fruits that they bear and have borne there? Where have they furthered and liberated human life? Where have they allowed a full, true life to succeed? Here is a critical (and indeed self-critical) testing of forms of faith. The Christian will measure these fruits by the Spirit of God, as God was in Jesus Christ. Here this criterion will itself become the object of dialogue.

Though ideal notions of the 'successful life' may depend on particular religious convictions, it is possible to note broad overlaps between them: at least in the negative definitions of what successful life is not.

The following three criteria have become important to me for testing faith by life as lived by the individual:

1. Does a form of faith also carry one through experiences of suffering? Does it do justice to the ambivalences of life, the unpredictable strokes of fate, human wickedness? Or does it turn into idealistic wishes and utopian dreams, which only flourish in a sub-tropical climate far from reality?

2. Does a form of faith break open what Luther called 'the heart

bent in on itself', open up men and women towards their environment and God, or is it primarily concerned with its own salvation? Does the way to God lead through others or past them? Does the form of faith also include the 'healing' of other life? Does it lead to mission as a 'universal diaconia',[42] or does it encourage a self-satisfied and selfish view of salvation?

This criterion can be taken further in two directions: (a) Is faith 'constructive' and does it contribute to the building up of the community of faith? and (b) Does it lead to liberating praxis in the 'world', to a commitment to justice and peace?

3. Has a form of faith integrated its own 'penultimacy' or does it vaunt itself as an ultimate truth which cannot be gone beyond? Does it therefore know that God not only gives it a foundation but also puts it radically in question? Does it understand itself as a *way*, or does it identify itself with God's truth and reality?

If we are concerned to test the spirits according to the flesh, the forms of faith by the way in which they are actually put to the test in life, then we shall see which of them are viable. A faith which tests itself in such a way has the right to be recognized by Christian participants in dialogue. But this does not end the encounter in dialogue – and also the dispute over the truth; it only opens it up.

So I am not arguing that we should refrain from judging other forms of faith and accepting indifferently all the special offers that come on the religious market. The confession of the presence of God in Jesus Christ forbids such indifference. Many growths which luxuriate in the 'jungle of the new religions'[43] need very critical examination, and some need sharp repudiation. However, I am arguing that a verdict should not be given before, but after, the dialogue, or, even better, in the dialogue. It is not a matter of refraining from defending Christian convictions to non-Christians. But such a defence should take place *dialogically*, and not as a recounting of truths which are fixed eternally and which the non-Christian does not yet know.

It can be said at least of the great world religions that the testing of forms of faith by life will show that a sweeping global judgment cannot be made either on the religions as a whole or even on one religion. In all religions there will be some phenomena which must be uncompromisingly rejected (like the calls to 'holy war' against those of another faith supported by religious motives), and others where we think that the Christian way is better (for example the assessment of the individual in his or her present life as compared with the Hindu view of the cycle of births). And there will be things that we may admire and feel to be an enrichment (as perhaps the deep spirituality of Zen meditation).

Moreover there will also be phenomena in Christianity which the non-Christian dialogue partners will reject uncompromisingly (for the Muslim, for example, the moral liberalism of Western Christianity) and others where they think that their own religion is superior to Christianity (for Buddhists, for example, in the case of the Christian personal image of God). And there will be things which they can admire and feel to be an enrichment (thus, for example, Hindus may admire the social commitment of Christians).

The reason why no verdict can be passed on a religion as a whole lies in the limitation of all our perspectives and their ties to a particular place. Each of the great world religions represents a whole world-view crystallized around a particular centre, i.e. an all-embracing way of experiencing and understanding the world and living in it. We can judge truth only from these perspectives and not independently of them. There is no bird's-eye view from which we could decide 'from above' on the legitimation of such global forms of life.[44] For this understanding of religion, it is as nonsensical to judge a religion as a whole to be true or false as it would be to want to judge another culture or another language true or false.

And even within the individual religions, true can only mean truthful, i.e. 'corresponding to the nature of the religion'. Here, however, there is always a multiplicity of true ways of believing which clearly differ from one another. There is a polyphony of truths.

Mutual testing of claims to truth in inter-religious dialogue is not without self-interest. It follows Paul's instructions: 'Test everything; hold fast to what is good' (I Thess.5.21). And, 'Whatever is true, whatever is honourable, whatever is just, whatever is pure, whatever is lovely, whatever is gracious . . . think about these things' (Phil.4.8). This is an attitude which was adopted by many theologians of the early church when they expressed the message of Christ in the Spirit of their time.

The experience of many Christians who have entered into serious dialogue with those of other religions is not the dilution of their own Christian faith but its enrichment and deepening; not a syncretistic mixing which blurs the contours, nor relativizing and a dissolution of identity, but the rediscovery of the special character of their own faith. Just as one gets to know one's own cultural conditioning in a new way when staying in another cultural circle, so the encounter with other religions leads to reflection on (which does not mean retreat into) one's own religious roots. Hitherto obscured aspects of the Christian tradition are called to mind afresh.

The 'authentic' aspect emerges more clearly precisely where one evaluates and recognizes the 'authentic' aspect of other modes of faith. Where does this special character of Christian faith lie?

The special character of Christianity

Certainly there is a whole series of essentials which one could list if one were seeking to indicate where the distinctivness, the essence, of Christian faith lies. I shall pick out two characteristics which have become important to me – not least in my encounters in religious dialogue.

The first of these links up with what I said earlier about the 'revelation of God'. It centres on the fact that God reveals himself and the way in which he does so.

God is the absolute who breaks through this absoluteness. God does not remain with himself, but breaks out of the self-sufficiency of what rests apathically in itself, 'goes out of himself'. God opens himself, shares himself, surrenders himself, enters into the world and history. God wants to make people open, to ground themselves in this ground. Where people allow themselves to be opened up and adopt an open attitude they will also become open to others and put themselves in a dialogical relationship with them.

In Isa.58.8f. salvation means 'the inter-relation of word and answer. Salvation is not described as a state of bliss, but as the constancy of the dialogical relationship between human beings and God (Buber)'.[45]

But when God shows himself to human beings, was it not and is it not a one-sided event? Does not everything stem from God, as Karl Barth constantly emphasized? Everything indeed stems from God, yet nevertheless revelation is not a one-sided event but a reciprocal giving and taking. In showing a creative and saving interest in the world in which human beings live, in the person of the Jew Jesus of Nazareth God takes upon himself the most profound human experience of life. God is not characterized by 'absolutist' rule with all the attributes of an untouchable Sun King, but by an attractive and threatening, active and suffering entanglement in the doings of creatures. God's dealings with the world are characterized by dialogue, not monologue. God's word does not decree but exposes itself to other words, seeking an answer. And conversely it takes up human discourse, life and suffering into itself and reacts to them. It is not the case that God alone is active and human beings are left only the role of passive recipients who react and respond. God acts and reacts, speaks and hears, does and suffers. So do human beings. Christians have to follow this structure in their dealings with those of other faiths.

Furthermore, since in Jesus God had human experiences to the point of suffering and dying, God become another God, one who is near and human, for whom salvation is not a Platonic idea beyond time which he has decreed universally once and for all, but a historical reality which has come about in a particular place in history and in so doing necessarily remains particular.

This confession of the deepest humiliation of God who has penetrated the ultimate depths of human suffering, this confession of the nearness of God and God's capacity for compassion, are among the greatest riches that Christians can contribute to dialogue. It is a light that must not be put under a bushel, but it must not quench all other lights as a triumphal truth. For that would be to betray the essence of 'lowliness christology' in the act, in the process of dialogue. Christianity itself also stands 'under the cross'.[46]

That brings me to the second feature which is characteristic of Christianity. The special nature of this religion lies in its deep realism. First of all, there is no flight from the world, no illusion about reality, no utopia. Secondly, there is no tie to the world, no being handed over to reality as it is now. Redemption means liberation from dependence on the things of the world without withdrawal from the world to an island of the blessed. Christianity does not bring redemption *from* the world but liberation *for* the world. This attitude is expressed in a concentrated way by Paul (in I Cor.7.29–31) where he invites his readers to have the things of this world as though they did not have them.

This detachment from the world makes possible a realism which does not sell itself to reality, which stands critically over against reality because it knows that in God's light it should be other than it is. The world must not and may not be rejected or forsaken, but it cannot remain as it is; it needs redemption. So Christians are aware of the ultimate relativity of all the conditions of the world without lapsing into apathetic relativism. 'Faith releases the Christian so that he can be independent of the world and at the same time puts him under the obligation to stand up to its testing.'[47] Detachment from the world and standing up in the world belong together.

The relationship of Christianity to the other religions and not least to itself is also part of this deep realism. First of all, that means that Christians can see the religions, without theological prejudices, as they really are – with all that is fascinating and repulsive about them. They can take the religions with the utmost seriousness in their manifestations and their claim to truth. Christians can also see Christianity without illusions as one religion among others, with all the entanglements in which it keeps getting involved, and also with the strength which it exerts to keep freeing itself from them.

Secondly, it means that the ultimate relativization of all that happens in the world also includes the ultimate relativization of all religion. The Pauline 'have as though one did not have' must also apply to the possession of religious truth. So we can say that the 'essence' of Christianity lies not least in its abandonment of all religious claims to absoluteness and all church claims to power (along with all other claims to absoluteness and power); these claims, too, stand under the sign of the cross. The cross becomes the symbol of judgment on all human claims to absolute truth and authority. Paul Tillich put it like this: there is no unconditional truth of faith – apart from the truth that no one possesses it.[48]

We have God's truth as a given which defends itself against all attempts to 'have' it, to claim it as one's own possession. We have the absolute revelation of God only in 'earthen vessels' (II Cor.4.7), in concrete (interpreted) experiences of history. We have it only as perspectivistic truth, never as objective, universal truth.

Christians are aware of being caught in the tension between judgment (cross) and promise (resurrection). They are not allowed to want to have the promise for themselves and to project the judgment on other religions – as Christian fundamentalists do.

Peoples of God on the way

'For all the peoples walk, each in the name of its God, but we will walk in the name of the Lord our God for ever and ever' (Micah 4.5).

John Hick describes the way of the religions through history in a parable:

We have been like a company of people marching down a long valley, singing our own songs, developing over the centuries our own stories and slogans, unaware that over the hill there is another valley, with another great company of people marching in the same direction, but with their own language and songs and stories and ideas; and over another hill yet another marching group – each ignorant of the existence of the others. But then one day they all come out onto the same plain, the plain created by modern global communications, and see each other and wonder what to make of one another. You might think that the different groups would then simply greet one another as fellow companies of pilgrims. But in fact that is made difficult by part of the content of our respective songs and stories. For if we are Christians, we have been singing for centuries that there is no other name given among men, whereby we may be saved, than the name of Jesus. And if we are Jews, we have been singing that we are God's only chosen people, a light to lighten the world. And if we are Muslims, we have been singing that Muhammad (peace be upon him) is the seal of the prophets, bringing God's latest and final revelation. And if we are Buddhists or Hindus, we have been singing yet other songs which imply that we have the highest truth while others have only lesser and partial truths.[49]

Christians are in God's truth and on the way to it. Being on the way has nothing to do with the 'absolutist' self-glorification and the supra-historical triumphalism which thinks itself already to be in possession of the truth. Rather, it involves the sober realism of a humble quest for truth in recollection of the truth that has already come to pass.

That Christians in God's truth are on the way to it does not exclude the possibility that men and women of other religions are on the way to it by other routes.

That does not mean that the other religions as such are 'ways to salvation'. From what perspective could one make such a judgment? Again this would have to be the absolutist perspective of the omniscient observer who was also certain that Christianity alone is the way to salvation. Just as it is an irresponsible, almost ideological, generalization to describe Christianity as the only true religion, so it is an equally nonsensical prejudice, because it is so utterly abstract, simply to set all religions side by side as ways to salvation.

By contrast, it seems to me to be meaningful and justified to suppose that God could find ways to human beings and human beings could find ways to God in each of the great religions which are rich in tradition, ways which transform and transcend their lives in a svaing way. John Hick has discovered and described a very similar basic process in all religions: the transformation from egocentrism to a relationship to that which is not the self, to the world around, to fellow human beings and ultimately to the ground of the world.[50]

It makes a great difference whether one says that the religions are ways to salvation or that there are ways to salvation in the religions. The latter statement takes account of the fact that there are also disastrous ways in the religions. Secondly, the latter statement takes seriously limitations of our perspectives. For the judgment we make is an empirical one (which grows out of encounter) and holds only 'as far as we can see'. And thirdly, the judgment is hypothetical. For a well-meaning presupposition which opens up dialogue has to demonstrate its truth in dialogue. It is not meant to be a theological judgment, but to show a possibility which is to be kept open, which reminds the consciousness that God's ways for us are ultimately unfathomable. This does not put the uniqueness of the Christian way to God in question, but only the claim that it is the only way.

However, openness to the possibility, indicated above, that God also finds ways to human beings in other religions and that human beings find ways to him has consequences for thought and action in Christian faith.

1. The claim to exclusiveness, to being the sole truth, holds *within* this faith; it is part of the unconditional certainty about the truth among Christians. But as such it remains related to faith and the confession. That means that to say 'Christ alone' is to say something about the Christian confession of Christ, not to state a universal

abstract truth 'about', but a personal testimony 'to'. True as it is that God's self-event in Jesus Christ holds good not only for Christians but for all men and women, it is also true that only to Christians does the fullness of the Spirit of God disclose itself solely in Christ. Of course this way is potentially open to all men and women, but those who do not take it need not necessarily be on the wrong way.

2. The claims to universality and finality are not to be related to the reality of Christianity within history, nor directly to the message of Christ. In them, attention is drawn to the end of the way of God with human beings. They are and remain promise. Referring to Joachim Jeremias, Joseph Ratzinger points out that 'in Jesus' own message universalism is ... pure promise', as in the Old Testament.[51] Theo Sundermeier points out that in Paul the universalism belongs in the doxologies.[52] We are still on the way to the comprehensive realization of the reality of God; it is provisionally given to us only as a hope, a pledge.

Understood in this way, the claim to universality and finality, and even the claim to exclusiveness, can be retained as an expression of the Christian certainty of faith, without lapsing into the absolutist attitude. It then contributes towards expressing the special character of the Christian faith without the need to repudiate the special features of other forms of faith.

But the Christian claim to absoluteness has its real place not in dialogue, but in praise of God, in doxology. Believers can and may speak in the superlatives of devotion in praise of the majesty of the creator, his creative and reconciling presence in the human world and his promise of a new heaven and a new earth. Language must go to its limits – and sometimes even beyond – in order to hint at the ineffable.

However, this terminology must not be confused with the factual language of the intellect which is used to describe or explain reality as it is. This is not the cool prose of reason, but the passionate poetry of the heart.[53] It is not a report, but devotional language, an expression of the absoluteness of God.

For that is all that the 'claim to absoluteness' can mean: that we do not claim absoluteness for our faith, but rather that the Absolute – God himself – lays claim on us as on his whole creation.

Postscript

At the end of this journey, which has led us through the Christian claim to absoluteness in history and the present, some readers may regret that – especially in the last chapter – I have kept too much on the level of theological reflection. I have not really entered into dialogue with the religions and sects, nor have I gone into those specific problems which often cause so many difficulties for participants, despite their good will. It has been my intention to use theology, which in its history has so often supported the claim to absoluteness, to prepare the ground for a dialogical encounter of the religions. I wanted to show that a dialogical imperative arises from the Christian faith itself, and in so doing I wanted to counter the uncertainty that can be detected among many Christians in this respect and to help them to feel free to approach people of another faith in dialogue.

I know how sobering the results of numerous attempts at dialogue have been and how they often end in frustration and mutual antipathy. Even so, to go on being aware of our ultimately indispensable fellowship – by suffering through one another – is an expression of belief in the Spirit of God which brings fellowship, whose influence does not end where fellowship breaks down but whose mission is rather to make men and women open to God's universal will for salvation, a mission which ultimately cannot be opposed by any theological demands and any religious claim to absoluteness.

Notes

Preface: Theology in the Service of Religious Peace

1. Hans Küng, the well-known Tübingen theologian, has drawn this conclusion: there will be no peace among the nations of this world without peace between the religions. And there will be no peace between the religions without a dialogue between them (in id., *Global Responsibility*, 1991, 108ff.; cf. also id. and K.-J. Kuschel [eds.], *A Global Ethic*, 1993).

2. C. F.von Weizsäcker, *Der Garten des Menschlichen. Beiträge zur geschichtlichen Anthropologie*, 1977, 519.

Introduction: Is There a 'Malignant Principle' in Christian Faith?

1. L. Feuerbach, *The Essence of Christianity*, reissued New York 1957, 252 (his italics). In his article 'Interreligiöse Hermeneutik in kirchlich-institutionellen Kontexten', in J. A. van der Ven and H. G. Ziebertz, *Interreligiöses Lernen*, 1994, the Mainz expert on religions, Andreas Grünschloss, writes: 'It is a fact of the study of religion that religious traditions and communities are almost "essentially" intransigent [i.e.irreconcilable] because of their relationship to the transcendent which they experience and think of in contingent terms' (39).

2. I have borrowed this term from Tertullian, who says of the divine wisdom that it is 'our weapon against spiritual enemies, all wickedness and fleshly desire, the sword which for the sake of God's name can cut us off even from those who are dearest to us' (*adversus Marcionem* III.14.3).

3. See A. Pithan, '500 Jahre Christentum in Lateinamerika. Herrschaft und Dialog', in R. Kirste, P. Schwarzenau, and U. Tworuschka (eds.), *Engel, Elemente, Energien*, Religionen im Gespräch 2, 1992, 89–92.

4. Quoted from L. and T. Engl, 'Das "Requerimiento". Vom "gerechten Krieg" gegen die Indios', in R. Beck (ed.), *1492. Die Welt zur Zeit des Kolumbus, Ein Lesebuch*, 1992, 207–12: 210f.

5. K. Jaspers, *Der philosophische Glaube*, 1948, ⁷1981, 69.

6. W. Pannenberg, 'Religion und Religionen. Theologische Erwägungen zu den Prinzipien eines Dialogs mit den Weltreligionen', in A. Bsteh (ed.), *Dialog*

aus der Mitte christlicher Theologie, 1987, 187.

7. H. Döring, 'Der universale Anspruch der Kirche und die nichtchristliche Religionen', *MTZ* 41, 1990, 78.

1. Radical Protestants – Three Examples

1. Thus Roman-Catholic dignitaries in spring 1990. Here and in what follows I am making use of C. J. Jäggi and D. J. Krieger, *Fundamentalismus. Ein Phänomen der Gegenwart*, 1991, 92–9.

2. M. Eckholt, in *HerKorr* 47, 1993, 250f. There is a comprehensive account in D. Martin, *Tongues of Fire. The Explosion of Protestantism in Latin America*, 1990.

3. J. Moltmann, 'Fundamentalism and Modernity', *Concilium* 1992/3, 115.

4. Quoted from Jäggi and Krieger, *Fundamentalismus* (n.1). For the situation in Guatemala see also H. Schäfer, *Befreiung vom Fundamentalismus. Entstehung einer neuen kirchlichen Praxis im Protestantismus Guatemalas*, 1988.

5. Cf. Jäggi and Krieger, *Fundamentalismus* (n.1), 75–81.

6. See *Bibel und Gemeinde* 79, 1979, 6ff.

7. See also the introduction to the German publication of the Chicago Declaration in *idea*, quoted in H. Haug, 'Fundamentalismus in der Religion. Bericht über die Jahrestagung 1991 des Bundes für Freies Christentum', *Religionen im Gespräch* (see Introduction, n.3).

8. Already in 1970 'Euro 70', a major rally with Billy Graham, was transmitted from Dortmund to more than thirty cities. The 'Informationsdienst der Evangelischen Allianz' (idea) was founded to support this rally.

2. Evangelicalism and Protestant Fundamentalism

1. P. Beyerhaus, 'Wesenmerkmale des nachchristlichen Synkretismus', *Diakrisis*, May 1991, 73f.

2. P. Beyerhaus, 'Der Dialog als Ausdruck eines neuen ökumenischen Missverständnisses', in id., *Krise und Neuaufbruch der Weltmission*, 1987, 101.

3. *Christliches Bekenntnis und biblischer Auftrag angesichts des Islam. Ein Wort der Konferenz Bekennender Gemeinschaften in evangelischen Kirchen Deutschlands und der AG evangelikaler Missionen* (1984), section V.

4. J. Barr, *Fundamentalism*, 1977; id., 'Fundamentalismus', in *EKL*[3] I, 1404–6. Here is a selection from a series of more recent publications on this topic: J. Niewiadowski (ed.), *Eindeutige Antworten? Fundamentalistische Versuchung in Religion und Gesellschaft*, 1988; C. Colpe and H. Papenthin (eds.), *Religiöser Fundamentalismus – Unverzichtbare Glaubensbasis oder ideologischer Strukturfehler?*, 1989; T. Meyer, *Fundamentalismus in der modernen Welt*, 1989; U. Birnstein, *'Gottes einzige Antwort ...' Christlicher Fundamentalismus im Vormarsch*, 1990; C. J. Jäggi and K. Kienzle (eds.), *Der neue Fundamentalismus*.

Rettung oder Gefahr für Gesellschaft und Religion?, 1990; H. Hemminger (ed.), *Fundamentalismus in der verweltlichten Kultur*, 1991; H. Kochanek, *Die verdrängte Freiheit. Fundamentalismus in den Kirchen*, 1991; G. Kepel, *Die Rache Gottes. Radikale Moslems, Christen und Juden auf dem Vormarsch*, 1991; G. Ramsden, *Understanding Fundamentalism and Evangelicalism*, 1991; J. Werbick (ed.), *Offenbarungsanspruch und Fundamentalistische Versuchung*, QD 129, 1991: M. Odermatt, *Der Fundamentalismus. Ein Gott – eine Wahrheit – eine Moral?*, 1992; H. Mynarek, *Denkverbot. Fundamentalismus in Christentum und Islam*, 1992.

5. Barr, 'Fundamentalismus' (n.7); M. Marquardt, 'Fundamentalismus', *TRT*[4] 2, 131–3; W. Joest, 'Fundamentalismus', *TRE* 11, 732–8.

6. F. Jung, *Die Deutsche Evangelikale Bewegung. Grundlinien ihrer Geschichte und Theologie*, EHS XXIII/461, 1992, 22; he gives a survey of the basic positions in Protestant theology on pp.179–216. See also F. Laubach and H. Stadelmann (eds.), *Was Evangelikale glauben. Die Glaubensbasis der Evangelischen Allianz erklärt*, 1989.

7. Point 1 of the 1846 Basis of Faith of the Evangelical Alliance.

8. Jung, *Deutsche Evangelikale Bewegung* (n.6), 180.

9. Ibid., 180ff.

10. See e.g. G. Maier, *Das Ende der historisch-kritischen Methode*, 1974.

11. Barr, *Fundamentalism* (n.4), 72ff.

12. This is an aspect of that often total opportunism which prevails in such groups. The members delegate their own autonomy to an authoritative person and thus regress into a childlike attitude in which they accept decisions made for them.

13. D. Seeber, 'Zurück an die Wurzeln', *HerKorr* 43, 1989, 2.

14. For Catholic fundamentalism in particular see W. Beinert (ed.), *Katholischer Fundamentalismus. Häretische Gruppen in der Kirche?*, 1991; H. Kochanek, *Die verdrängte Freiheit* (n.4), especially ch.2; S. Pfürtner, 'Traditionalistische Bewegungen in gegenwärtigen Katholizismus', in R. Frieling (ed.), *Die Kirchen und ihre Konservativen*, Bensheimer Hefte 62, 1984, 1151; P. Hebblethwaite, 'A Fundamentalist Pope?', *Concilium* 1992/3, 88–96.

15. *KNA–ID* no.26 of 28 June 1990, 2.

16. W. Gitt, *Das biblische Zeugnis der Schöpfung*, 154.

17. Quoted in Jäggi and Krieger, *Fundamentalismus* (Ch.1, n.1),79.

3. Religious 'Absolutism' as an Attitude and a Pattern of Behaviour

1. 'Die Sehnsucht nach dem Absoluten, nach sicherem Grund', a lecture given in Zurich, 1990, quoted in Jäggi and Krieger, *Fundamentalismus* (see ch.1, n.1), 40.

2. In the following description I draw on the results of research into ideologies and fundamentalism, and peace studies. The classics of these

disciplines include: T. W. Adorno, E. Frenkel-Brunswik and D. J. Levinson, *The Authoritarian Personality*, 1950; T. W. Adorno, *Studien zum autoritären Charakter*, 1973; M. Rokeach, *The Open and Closed Mind*, 1960.

3. H. Albert, *Traktat über kritische Vernunft*, [2]1969, 33f.

4. Cf. the definition of fundamentalism by S. Pfürtner: 'Fundamentalism is the attempt to spare people in their longing for security and safety the venture of faith and instead offer them the *pseudo-security* of a fixed, unchangeable sphere, or one protected by authority' ('Katholische Theologen sprechen über den katholischen Fundamentalismus. Ängstliche Lebensphilosophie', *KIPA*, 9 February 1989, quoted in Jäggi and Krieger, *Fundamentalismus* (see Ch.1, n.1), 25f.

5. M. E. Marty, 'What is Fundamentalism? Theological Perspectives', *Concilium* 1992/3, 5.

6. Thus E. Gelbach, in *Erwachsenenbildung* 1/1992, 9ff., and id., 'Evangelismus. Versuch eine historischen Typologie', in R. Frieling (ed.), *Die Kirchen und ihre Konservativen* (see Ch.2, n.3), 63, following G. M. Marsden, *Fundamentalism and American Culture. The Shaping of Twentieth-Century Evangelicalism 1870–1925*, 1980, 113.

7. Thus G. Sauter writes in his introduction to the German edition of James Barr's *Fundamentalism*: 'In its incessant objections to "modern science" the fundamentalist ideology fails to recognize how dependent it is on that science itself – but only in a particular stage which has meanwhile been overtaken by science itself, namely the ultimately uncritical rationalism of the first Enlightenment, though this has continued beyond the nineteenth century, above all in the natural sciences. Fundamentalism shares with this rationalism the longing for a complete world view which combines all information in itself' (*Fundamentalismus*, 1981, 10f.).

8. P. Watzlawick, *Münchhausens Zopf oder: Psychotherapie und Wirklichkeit*, 1992, 225.

9. 'The idea of being in possession of the ultimate truth first of all leads to a messianic attitude which clings to the belief that the truth will automatically establish itself *qua* truth. At this point the defender of an ideology perhaps still believes it possible to instruct or convince the heretic. But as the world soon proves to be stubborn, unwilling or incapable of openness to the truth, the next necessary step is what Herman Lübbe calls the ideological self-enablement to power. The eyes of the world must be opened in its own best interests' (ibid., 206f.).

10. Haug, *Fundamentalismus in der Religion* (Ch.1, n.7), 459.

11. According to E. W. Russell, 'Christianity and Militarism', *Peace Research Review* IV.3, November 1971.

12. Helmut Langel, quoted in Haug, 'Fundamentalismus in der Religion' (Ch.1, n.7), 461.

13. R. A. Mall, 'Wahrheit und Toleranz als hermeneutisches Problem',

Dialog der Religionen 3, 1993, 32. H. Zirker offers a summary of basic fundamentalist attitudes which can also be taken as a summary of what I have said about the 'absolutist' attitude: 'Narrow orientations on an enlightened past, the dominance of thought in terms of security, a regressive retreat into one's own group, protection of the consciousness against alien irritations, a zealous quest for reciprocal self-confirmation, a high value attached to uniformity, suspicions about doubt and criticism, simplifications which shy off the problem, the aggressive repudiation of other positions, making authorities tabu' ('Geschichtliche Offenbarung und Endgültigkeitsansprüche. Voraussetzungen des Fundamentalismus in Christentum und Islam', in J. Werbick [ed.], *Offenbarungsanspruch und fundamentalistische Versuchung*, QD 129, 1991, 182).

4. *The Claim to Absoluteness – Support for the Self in Inner Uncertainty*

1. M. Marty, 'Fundamentalism as a Social Phenomenon', in G. Marsden, *Evangelicalism and Modern America*, 1984, 58.
2. Fritz Riemann, *Grundformen der Angst*, [4]1969. The following account is part of a lecture which I gave in 1991 at the Evangelische Akademie at Loccum and which appeared, slightly abbreviated, under the title 'Der Absolutheitsanspruch des Christentum', *Deutsches Pfarrerblatt* 91, 1991, 405–8.
3. I. Rudin, *Fanatismus*, [5]1975, mentions as characteristics of the schizoid personality structure: 'psychological rigidity in thoughts and ideas', 'narrow emotions', 'total identification with the idea . . . to the bitter end'.
4. James W. Fowler, *Stages of Faith*, 1981; id., *Faith Development and Pastoral Care*, 1987; id., Karl Ernst Nipkow and Friedrich Schweitzer, *Stages of Faith and Religious Development*, 1992.

5. *The Claim to Absoluteness – A Spiritual Refuge in Outward Uncertainty*

1. W. Philipp in his introduction to the text which he edited, *Das Zeitalter der Aufklärung*, reprinted 1988, XXXIX.
2. M. Geiger, cited by Philipp, *Das Zeitalter der Aufklärung*, XLVII.
3. For the Reformers it was not the individual words of scripture as such which were the Word of God; these words had to be understood in the light of Christ as the living Word of God (and hence could even be criticized). God's Word was *in, with and under* the letters of the Bible. By contrast, the doctrine of the literal dictation of the biblical texts identifies the 'content', the subject of revelation, with the *written* revelation and thus puts the whole content of Holy Scripture on the same level.
4. Philipp, *Das Zeitalter der Aufklärung* (n.1), XLVIf.
5. The last words of the late Ayatollah Khomeini clearly attest this: 'Muslims of the world, the disinherited of the earth, arise, and fight for your rights with claws and teeth. Do not fear the cries of the superpowers! Drive out your

tyrannical rulers who give the fruits of your labour to your enemy and the enemies of Islam. Take the destinies of your countries into your own hands. Unite under the proud banner of Islam and establish Islamic rule with independent and free republics. In this way you will strip the powerful on earth of their power and the barefooted will be the lords of the earth' (quoted in Jäggi and Krieger, *Fundamentalismus* [Ch.1, n.1], 100).

6. I have taken the following description of Islamic fundamentalism from Jäggi and Krieger, *Fundamentalismus* (see Ch.1, n.1), 100–16.

7. M. S. Abdullah, 'What Shall be the Answer to Contemporary Islamic Fundamentalism?', *Concilium* 1992/3, 76. Similarly B. Tibi, *Die fundamentalistische Herausforderung. Der Islam und die Weltpolitik*, 1992, according to whom the Islamic fundamentalist is 'not a *homo religiosus* but a political activist'.

8. According to Nancy Ammermann, whose investigation is reported by John Coleman, 'Global Fundamentalism: Sociological Perspectives', *Concilium* 1992/3, 39f.

6. The Claim to Absolute Truth – A Bulwark in the Battle of Faith

1. Large parts of Karl Barth's theology are to be understood in terms of this confrontation, i.e. contextually. In his book *Versöhnung und Befreiung*, which appeared in 1993, Berthold Klappert makes interesting 'attempts to understand Karl Barth contextually' (thus the subtitle).

2. *Church Dogmatics* IV/3.1, 1961, 151ff.

7. The Roots of the Christian Claim to Absoluteness in the Separation from Judaism

1. But see also already Isa 56.3–8, where the deciding factor for membership of the people of God is obedience to the God of Israel and no longer birth.

2. R. Ruether, *Faith and Fratricide. The Theological Roots of Antisemitism*, 1974, 56.

3. None of the New Testament authors yet transfers the name "Israel" explicitly to the Christian church except in Gal.6.16. But when Paul speaks of "Israel according to the flesh" (I Cor.10.18) and Revelation attacks "those who say that they are Jews and are not" (2.9; 3.9), both are manifestly also thinking of another "Israel", of the real Jews, . . . i.e. of the church' (M. Simon, 'Israel im NT und in der Alten Kirche', *RGG*³, 3, 946).

4. See Rom.9–11, where Paul (in 11.17–24), using the image of the olive tree, describes the Gentile Christians as a branch which was grafted on to the trunk of Israel. However, this is not a claim to any lasting significance for the 'old Sinai covenant'; that is superseded once and for all.

5. Tertullian, *Adversus Judaeos* 1–3; *Apostolic Constitutions* VII. 36.2; *Didaskalia* II.26.2.

6. Ruether, *Faith and Fratricide* (n.2), 78.

7. See also Paul in II Cor.3.4ff. *Kerygma Petri*, composed around 100 CE, states: 'A new (covenant) has he (God) made with us. For what has reference to the Greeks and Jews is old. But we are Christians, who as a third race worship him in a new way' (W. Schneemelcher [ed.], *New Testament Apocrypha* 2, ²1992, 39).

8. Ruether, *Faith and Fratricide* (n.2), 258.

9. Quoted from R. Heiligenthal, 'Ist der "Antijudaismus" konstitutiv für das Christentum? Zum sogenannter Antijudaismus im Johannesevangelium', *Deutsches Pfarrerblatt* 92, 1992, 189.

10. A. von Harnack, *The Expansion of Christianity in the First Three Centuries*, 1904, 81. There is a vivid description of this process of separation between Christians and Jews in Léon Poliakov, 'Der Antisemitismus während der ersten Jahrhunderte des Christentums', in id., *Geschichte des Antisemitismus*, Vol.1, 1977, 15–23.

11 R. Bultmann, *Theology of the New Testament*, Vol.1, 1952, 22f.

12. Ibid., 22.

13. See Poliakov, *Geschichte des Antisemitismus* (8 vols), 1977ff.

14. See n.4.

8. 'Claims to Absoluteness' in the Bible

1. J. Becker, *Das Evangelium nach Johannes*, ÖTK.NT 4/1, ³1991, 104.

2. K. Wengst, *Bedrängte Gemeinde und verherrlichter Christus*, 1991.

3. H. Thyen, 'Johannesevangelium', *TRE* 17, 212.

4. H. Gollwitzer, 'Ausser Christus kein Heil? (Johannes 14.6)', in W. P. Eckert, N. P. Levinson and M. Stöhr (eds.), *Antijudaismus im Neuen Testament?*, 1967, 173.

5. Ibid., 194.

6. 'Because Christianity developed from the Jewish tradition of faith not only in terms of religious history but above all theologically, and formed its own profile against this, the "anti-Judaistic" motifs in the New Testament are essential to Christian theology' (U. Wilckens, 'Das Neue Testament und die Juden. Antwort an David Flusser', *EvTh* 34, 1974, 611).

7. If anti-Judaism is essential to Christian theology, how can it be possible really to prevent the 'fusing of this anti-Judaism with antisemitisms of all kinds' – as Wilckens requires? With what justification can one then follow his appeal 'to guard against any condemnation of the Jewish people on a religious basis?' (ibid.).

8. A. H. J. Gunneweg, *Geschichte Israels bis Bar Kochba*, ⁴1982, 132.

9. Ibid.

10. Becker, *Evangelium des Johannes* (n.1), 69.

11. See also 1.9; 7.7; 8.12; 12.15, 35, 46; 15.12–25; 17.13; I John 1.7; 2.9,

11, 15; 3.10–15.

12. Ruether, *Faith and Fratricide* (see Ch.7, n.2), 114.

13. F. Rosenzweig, *Briefe*, 1935, 311.

14. Jesus' interest is 'in the judgment on Israel and not in the salvation of the Gentiles and its possibility' (N. A. Dahl, *Das Volk Gottes*, 1963, 150). Most exegetes do not regard the so-called mission command in Matt.28 as a saying of the historical Jesus, but attribute it to the Hellenistic–Jewish Christian communities, which wanted to provide a theological foundation for their missionary activity. In Matt.10.5f. Jesus forbids his disciples even to preach to the Gentiles.

15. I use the term 'pagan(s)' here and elsewhere as a value–neutral term for all those who are neither Christians nor Jews.

16. E. Haenchen, *The Acts of the Apostles*, 1971, 217.

17. Cf. Paul in I Cor.3.11.

18. K.-J.Kuschel, 'Christologie und interreligiöser Dialog. Die Einzigartigkeit Christi im Gespräch mit den Weltreligionen', *STZ* 116, 1991, 387–420. The page numbers in square brackets refer to this text. See also id., *Born Before All Time? The Dispute over Christ's Origin*, 1992, 327–39.

19. G. Ebeling, 'Schrift und Erfahrung als Quelle theologischer Aussagen', *ZTK* 75, 1978, 103.

9. *The Roots of the Christian Claim to Absoluteness in the Fight against Hellenistic Syncretism*

1. See K. Rudolph, *Gnosis*, 1992.

2. See the Isis aretalogies, and D. Müller, *Ägypten und die Isis Aretalogien*, 1961. For syncretism in late antiquity see M. P. Nilsson, *Geschichte der griechischen Religion*, Vol.2, Handbuch der Altertumswissenschaft, 5.2, 555–672.

3. Plutarch, *de Iside*, 377F; also in Celsus: see Origen, *Contra Celsum*, I.24 and V.41.

4. Plutarch, *Quaest.conviv.* IV.6.

5. Antiochus Epiphanes.

6. See also Chapter 16, n.30.

7. Apuleius, *Metamorphoses, or the Golden Ass*, Book XI: 'The Initiation of Lucius into the Mysteries of Isis and Osiris'.

8. See e.g. Lactantius, *Divine Institutions*, II.16.6f.

9. A. von Harnack, *What is Christianity?*, reissued 1957, 207 (his italics).

10. Ibid., 208.

11. This makes a decisive change to the Pauline 'dualism' of the two 'ages' (the old age in which men and women live according to the flesh and the new age in which they are in the Spirit or in Christ): the dynamic chronological overlapping of two realms has become a static juxtaposition of them.

12. See further Chapter 15.

13. The so-called pluralistic theologians of religion, see R. Bernhardt, *Horizontüberschreitung. Die Pluralistische Theologie der Religionen*, 1991; id., 'Ein neuer Lessing? – Paul Knitters Theologie der Religionen', *EvTh* 49, 1989, 516–28.

14. Thus the Bremen pastor G. Huntemann: 'Like many other Christians, I feel challenged by a Christianity of assimilation, i.e. one which does not resist the demonic character of our age but adapts to it in an almost abhorrent way' (quoted by H. Haug, 'Fundamentalismus in der Religion' [Ch.1, n.7], 458).

15. See also H. K. Chung, *Struggle to be the Sun Again. Introducing Asian Women's Theology*, 1990.

16. See also EMW (ed.), *Evangelium und Kultur. Eine Lese– und Arbeitsbuch für Gemeinde und Unterricht*, 1993: K. Raiser, 'Zur Gefahr des "Synkretismus" im Dialog der Religionen und Kulturen', *Wort und Antwort* 32, 1991, 12–7.

17. In his preface to R. Bäumer et al. (ed.), *Weg und Zeugnis. Bekennende Gemeinschaften im gegenwärtigen Kirchenkampf*, 1980, 2. See also the updating of the Barmen Theological Declaration by W.Künneth which was approved by the Fifth European Confessing Convention in Wuppertal-Barmen on 20–22 September 1984 (reprinted in H.Steubing [ed.], *Bekenntnisse der Kirche. Bekenntnistexte aus zwanzig Jahrhunderten*, 1985, 287ff.). The 'happenings and powers, images and truths', fought against in the first thesis of the 1934 Barmen Declaration, are said to encounter us today in the 'so-called theologies of liberation or feminism . . . in the form of an atheistic world humanism' or 'enthusiastic ideals of religious unity'.

18. In his 'Toward a Theology of the History of Religions', W. Pannenberg (*Basic Questions in Theology* 2, 1971, 270), wrote: 'Christianity, however, affords the greatest example of syncretistic assimilative power. This religion not only linked itself to Greek philosophy, but also inherited the entire religious tradition of the Mediterranean world – a process whose details have still not been sufficiently clarified, but which was probably decisive for the persuasive power of Christianity in the ancient world' (87).

19. F.-W. Haack, *Europas neue Religion. Sekten, Gurus, Satanskult*, 1993. See also the publications of the Evangelical Central Office for Ideological Questions in Stuttgart.

20. G. Essen, 'Die Wahrheit ins Spiel bringen. Bemerkungen zur gegenwärtigen Diskussion um eine Theologie der Religionen', *Pastoralblatt* 44, 1992, 138.

21. This consolidation of a defensive attitude has some similarities to the 'Schumpeter effect'. In 1919 Joseph Schumpeter described the autonomy of military complexes of rearmament. They are constructed against a temporary threat and develop a dynamic of their own which prevents disarmament once the danger has faded. So they continue without a function (see U. Horstmann, *Das Untier. Konturen einer Philosophie der Menschenflucht*, 1985, 62f.).

22. von Harnack, *What is Christianity?* (n.9), 125.

10. From the Claim to Absoluteness to State Control

1. K. Heussi, *Kompendium der Kirchengeschichte*, [15]1979, 92. To stem the attacks, in 423 CE an edict had to be issued in which the Christians were forbidden to 'lay hands on Jews or pagans'.

2. *De errore profanarum religionum.*

3. Theodosius, *Cunctos populos*, XVI 1.2.

4. Between 1861 and 1867 K. Werner collected in a five-volume work the apologetic and polemic literature which Christian theology has produced in its history (reprinted 1966).

5. H. F. von Campenhausen, *The Fathers of the Latin Church*, 1964, 17.

6. *Apology* 1.

7. *Apology* 24.2.

8. von Campenhausen, *The Fathers* (n.5), 17.

9. Ibid., 24.

10. *De praescriptione* 37.

11. *De praescriptione* 7.

12. Ibid.

13. *De unitate* 6. *Ep.* 74.7 reads: 'He who would have God as Father must first have the church as mother.'

14. *Ep.* 73.21.

15. *De unitate* 23.

16. Thus J. Baer in his introduction to *De unitate*, BKV 34, 126.

17. For the history of this statement see J. Brosseder, 'Die anonymen Christen', in H. Fries et al., *Heil in den Religionen und im Christentum*, Kirche und Religionen 2, 1982, 243–70: 245–51.

18. Quoted from *Epitome* 44. Cf. also *Divine Institutions*, Book IV ('The true wisdom and piety').

19. Ibid., 54ff.

20. H. von Soden, *Urkunden zur Entstehungsgeschichte des Donatismus*, [2]1950, no.23.

21. We shall meet such 'milder' judgments in Chapter 13.

22. J. C. Perl in his introduction to the German edition of *De vera religione*, 1957, XV.

23. *De vera religione* 5, closing sentence.

24. Following A. Adam, *Lehrbuch der Dogmengeschichte* I, [4]1981, 294–6.

25. But there are also statements in Augustine in which he makes this identification, e.g. *En. in Ps.* 98.4.

26. We shall be pursuing this further in Chapter 13.

27. 'The holy and ecumenical synod has decreed that it is unlawful for anyone to present, write, compose, devise or teach to others any other creed.'

28. As rendered in the 1662 Anglican *Book of Common Prayer*.
29. Adam, *Lehrbuch der Dogmengeschichte* (n.24 above), 296.

11. The Claim to Absoluteness – The Foundation for the Theology of the Crusades

1. See E. Benz, 'Ideen zu einer Theologie der Religionsgeschichte', in *Akademie der Wissenschaften und der Literatur. Abhandlungen der geistes– und sozialwissenschaftlichen Klasse*, 5, 1960, 442.
2. John of Nikiu, the first Christian theologian to pass judgment on Islam, describes the religion of Muhammad as 'a faith of the beast', God's punishment on the Eastern church which has forsaken the orthodox faith (according to G. Mensching, *Der offene Tempel. Die Weltreligionen im Gespräch miteinander*, 1974, 85).
3. For him, Islam 'misleads the nations' (B. Kotter, *Die Schriften des Johannes von Damaskus*, IV: *Liber de haeresibus*, PTS XXII, 1981, chs.100f.). See D. J. Sahas, *John of Damascus on Islam. The Heresy of the Ishmaelites*, 1972.
4. Quoted from R. Mokrosch and H. Walz, *Kirchen– und Theologiegeschichte in Quellen*, II, ²1986, 70.
5. Ibid.
6. Ibid., 71.
7. For the controversy between Christianity and Islam in the Middle Ages and in modern times see the account compiled by L. Hagemann in *Verkündigung und Forschung* 32, 1987, 43–62, with a full bibliography.
8. H. Kühner, *Das Imperium der Päpste*, 1980, 137.
9. Quotoed in Mokrosch and Walz, *Quellen* (n.4), 158.
10. Denziger, 1351, 342.
11. The Reformation formulae *sola gratia, sola fide, sola scriptura* are countered with a *sola ecclesia* (I.10.143, cf. I.10.16).
12. II.7.25.
13. Denzinger 3074, 601.

12. Solus Christus. *The Claim to Absoluteness in Martin Luther and Karl Barth*

1. WA 40.1, 603.19–606.31. In his Table Talk Luther had said: 'All religions which conflict with the true Christian religion are *ex opere operato* (i.e. are automatic): I want to do that, that will be well pleasing to God. By contrast one must maintain the principle that any work done of itself is idolatry' (WA, *Tischreden* 5, no.5505).
2. In *Bekenntnisschriften der evangelisch-lutherischen Kirche*, ⁵1963, 661.
3. *WA* 40.1, 609. In *EA* 46.29 he writes: 'if all . . . venerable pagans came before God with their precious virtues and actions, all their action would be sheer disgrace, lies and hypocrisy.'

4. The following account and the page numbers in square brackets in the text relate to Karl Barth, *Church Dogmatics* I/2, 1956. See R. Bernhardt, *Der Absolutheitsanspruch des Christentums. Von der Aufklärung bis zur Pluralistischen Religionstheologie*, ²1993, 149–73.

13. The Other Way: Inclusive Absoluteness

1. 'Logos' is the eternal, creative, primal word of God which manifests itself as the reason, the principle, the structure of the world.

2. Justin, *Apology* I.5.

3. *Apology* II.10 (my italics).

4. *Apology* I.46 (my italics).

5. 'Those who live in accord with the Logos are Christians, even if they are regarded as godless, like Socrates and Heraclitus among the Greeks, and Abraham, Ananias, Azarias, Misael and Elijah among the barbarians' (Justin, *Apology* I, 46.)

6. *Apology* II, 13.

7. In *Apology* 17.6 he speaks of the 'testimony (to the truth) of the soul which is naturally Christian (*testimonium animae naturaliter Christianae*)'.

8. *Stromateis* I.5.

9. Augustine, *Retractationes* I,123,3. See also *Ep.* 102.5.

10. Abelard, *Theologia Christiana*: Migne, *Patrologia Latina* 178, 1172.

11. Aquinas, *Summa theologiae*, II.II, 2.7 ad 3.; *Quaest. disp. de veritate* 14, 11 ad 5.

12. *Summa theologiae* I. 8 ad 2.

13. *Summa theologiae* I,II, 109 1 ad 1.

14. *'una religio in rituum varietate'* (*De pace fidei* 6, in Opera omnia VII, 7).

15. 'Declaration on the Relation of the Church to Non-Christian Religions' (*Nostra aetate*), no.2.

16. Ibid., no.3.

17. Declaration on Religious Liberty (*Dignitatis humanae*), no.1.

18. Above all *Theological Investigations*, 5, 1966, 115–34.

14. The Absoluteness of Christianity and the History of Religion

1. G. E. Lessing, *Nathan the Wise*, line 2050.

2. For the approaches of Schleiermacher and Hegel see R. Bernhardt, *Der Absolutheitsanspruch* (Ch.12, n.4), 807.

3. Quotations from *The Absoluteness of Christianity* (1912), 1972. The numbers in square brackets refer to this text.

4. K. Jaspers, *Der philosophische Glaube*, 1948. The numbers in square brackets refer to this text.

5. G. Mensching, *Vergleichende Religionswissenschaft*, ²1949, 161.

Notes

6. G. Mensching, 'Der Absolutheitsanspruch des Christentums im Vergleich mit den ausserchristlichen Weltreligionen', *US* 30, 1975, 42.

7. Ibid., 'Absolutheitsanspruch', 48; cf. *Vergleichende Religionswissenschaft*, 164.

8. H. Halbfas adopts this interpretation, and takes it even further. He sees the origin of the claim to absoluteness in the transformation from mythical to logical truth. Truth which is beyond human control, as manifested in myth, rite and symbol, is objectified, made finite and thus idolized (*Fundamentalkatechetik, Sprache und Erfahrung im Religionsunterricht,* ²1969, 230–7). He writes: 'It is not good for religions to misinterpret a legend as history, a metaphor as a concept, a myth as a doctrinal statement'.

9. F. M. Dostoievsky, *The Brothers Karamazov*, 1958, I, 298 (translation by David Magarshack).

15. Claims to Absoluteness in the Religions

1. F. Heiler, *Das Gebet,* ⁵1923, 255–8.

2. 'Hinduism' is a vague collective name for the religions of Inida coined by Europeans.

3. According to Jäggi and Krieger, *Fundamentalismus* (Ch.1, n.1), 134.

4. H. Küng, *Christianity and the World Religions*, 1986, 263f.

5. In the words of M. Horkheimer and T. W. Adorno, 'To approach something like the absolute of the finite, the finite is absolutized' (*Dialectic of the Enlightenment*, 1973, 186).

6. Küng, *Christianity and the World Religions* (n.4), 177.

7. G. von Rad, quoted by H. Gollwitzer, *Ausser Christus kein Heil?* (see Ch.8,n.4), 181.

8. Cf. also Isa.19.25.

9. Rabbi E. Berkowitz, quoted by S. J. Samartha, 'Mission in einer religiös pluralen Welt', in R. Bernhardt, *Horizontüberschreitung* (see Ch.9, n.13), 199.

10. Quoted from S. E. Karff, 'What Shall be the Answer to Contemporary Jewish Fundamentalism?', *Concilium* 1992/3, 57.

11. P. Lapide, 'Judentum – Christentum – Islam. Ein Gespräch', in B. Rübenach (ed.), *Begegnungen mit den Judentum*, 1981, 285.

12. These references and others in brackets are to the Qur'an.

13. Surah 3.20 reads: 'The only true faith in God's sight is Islam.'

14. 'He that chooses a religion other than Islam, it will not be accepted from him, and in the world to come he will be one of the lost' (3.87). 'As for the unbelievers, whether you forewarn them or not, they will not have faith. God has set a seal upon their hearts and ears; their sight is dimmed and a grievous punishment awaits them' (2.7f.). There are even sharper verdicts on unbelievers in 8.22f. and 8.5.

15. M. S. Abdullah, *Islam für das Gespräch mit Christen*, 1992, 136.

16. Ibid., 14.

17. *Die Glaubenslehren des Islam*, 1962, 77f.

18. Abdullah, *Islam für das Gespräch mit Christen* (n.15), 13.

19. The roots of the two words are related.

20. 'There shall be no compulsion in religion. True guidance is now distinct from error' (2.257).

21. Gandhi, quoted in Mensching, 'Der Absolutheitsanspruch des Christentums' (Ch.14, n.6), 40f.

22. Radhakrishnan, quoted in ibid., 41.

23. Quoted in H. Halbfas, *Religion*, 1976, 129f. This is a free translation: other authors render 'religion' as 'sect'.

24. The parable appears first in the Pali canon, then spread to India and entered the teaching of Persian Sufism. For what follows see also R. Bernhardt, 'Interreligiöse Bilder und Gleichnisse', *Dialog der Religionen* 3, 1993, 64–79.

25. *Udana* VI.4, quoted in K. Seidenstücker, *Udana, Das Buch der feierlichen Worte des Erhabenen*, nd, 77.

26. Sayings of the Buddha.

27. Quoted in T. Ohm, *Asiens Kritik am abendländischen Christentum*, 1949, 33.

28. Ibid., 37, quotes the Zen master Joka: 'One and the same moon is reflected in all waters. All the moons in the water are one with the one moon'.

29. T. Ohm, *Indien und Gott*, 1932, 257, attributes it to the Hindu woman Sarojini Naidu.

30. This is the answer of Genghis Khan's Enkel Mangu to a Franciscan monk who wanted to convert him to Christianity as the only true religion. See H. von Glasenapp, *Die fünf grossen Religionen*, II, 1952, 519f.

31. Cf. R. Rolland, *The Life of Ramakrishna*, 1929, 86. See also Mahendra Nath Gupta (ed.), *The Gospel of Sri Ramakrishna* II, 248. Here is another parable of Ramakrishna's, quoted from G. Mensching, *Der offene Tempel*, 182: 'Just as one can get to the roof of a house by a ladder or a bamboo stave or a staircase or a rope, so too there are different ways of reaching God, and each religion of the world shows one of these ways.' 'The Colour of the Chameleon', another of Ramakrishna's parables, has been included in M. and U. Tworuschka (ed.), *Fremde Religionen*, II, 1988, 424f.

32. This does not exclude the possibility of this claim also being made in them. Here are two examples. In Japan the school of Nichiren (Zen nichimero, 1222–1282) represented an aggressive trend of political Buddhism. Amida Buddhism was particularly condemned. A prayer of Amida was said to be the 'way to hell', which would be punished with a thousand years of purgatory. Nowadays the Nichiren sect has almost ten million adherents in Japan. In Hinduism, Dayanand Sarasvati (1824–1883) founded the Arya Samaj, the 'Community of Aryans', who made a strong claim to exclusiveness in defence against Christian influences. He regarded the Vedas as 'binding universal revelation for the whole of humankind' (O. Wolff, *Christus unter Hindus*, 1965,

108), and the other religions as apostasy from it.

33. Phra Khantipalo, *Tolerance: A Study from Buddhist Sources*, 1964, 114.

34. According to G. Rosenkranz, 'Was müssen wir heute unter Absolutheit des Christentums verstehen', *ZTK* 51, 1954, 113.

35. Quoted in T. Ohm, *Asiens Kritik*, 1949, 42.

36. H. J. Margull, 'Der "Absolutheitsanspruch" des Christentums im Zeitalter des Dialogs. Einsichten in der Dialogerfahrung', in J. Brantschen and P. Selvatico (eds.), *Unterwegs zur Einheit, FS H. Stirnmann*, 1980, 877.

37. P. Tillich, *The Protestant Era*, 1951, xliiif.

38. According to H. Zahrnt, *Die Sache mit Gott*, ⁵1982, 384.

39. Not even in Islam, as is shown by numerous renewal movements which have arisen since the nineteenth century. For brief information see F. Heiler, *Die Religionen der Menschheit*, 1959, 870ff.; H. Küng, *Christianity and the World Religions* (n.4), 97.

16. A Very Different Way: Christianity without a Claim to Absoluteness

1. Quoted from H. J. Margull (ed.), *Zur Sendung der Kirche – Material der ökumenischen Bewegung*, 1963, 13f.

2. Quoted from *epd-dokumentation* 16/91, 43f.

3. The following texts are quoted from the provisional translation by R. Kirste, in R. Kirste, P. Schwarzenau and U. Tworuschka (eds.), *Gemeinsam vor Gott. Religionen in Gespräch*, 1991, 229–35. The page numbers in square brackets refer to this translation.

4. Professor Vasvani stated there: 'The world religions are not rivals, but they are brothers. Why do we not band together and form a family of faith to the honour of the Father, who is at work in all?' (quoted from G. Mensching, 'Religionskongresse', *RGG*³, 5, 995f.).

5. What Pope John Paul II said when he was enthroned in October 1978 echoes the words of J. R. Mott in Edinburgh cited above: 'Open wide the doors for Christ. To his saving power open the boundaries of states, economic and political systems, the vast fields of culture, civilization and development. Do not be afraid' (quoted from Peter Hebblethwaite, 'A Fundamentalist Pope?', *Concilium* 1992/3, 89). Like John R. Mott, so too John Paul II is concerned with the (re-)evangelization of the world in the next few years. Just as the North American fundamentalists wanted to create (or more precisely restore) a 'Christian America' in the 1920s, so the pope envisages Russia once again as a 'Christian Russia' and Poland as a 'Christian Poland'. Here we have a sign of the integralism which was already mentioned in Chapter 2.

6. J. Zehner, *Der notwendige Dialog. Die Weltreligionen in katholischer und evangelischer Sicht*, Studien zum Verstehen fremder Religionen 3, 1992, 65.

7. See Chapter 13.

8. Quoted from H.-W. Gensichen, 'Christen im Dialog mit Menschen

anderen Glaubens. Ökumenische Studienkonferenzen in Kandy (Ceylon), 10.2 – 6.3.1967', *EMZ* 24, 1967, 83.

9. See H. J. Margull and S. J. Samartha (eds.), *Dialog mit anderen Religionen. Materialien aus der ökumenischen Bewegung*, 1972.

10. The development of the idea of dialogue in the ecumenical movement is sketched out by G. Rosenstein, *Die Stunde des Dialogs. Begegnung der Religionen heute*, Pädagogische Beiträge zur Kulturbegegnung, Vol.9, 1991, 44–105; Zehner, *Der notwendige Dialog* (n.6), 65–112; A. Grünschloss, *Interreligiöse Hermeneutik in kirchlich-institutionellen Kontexten* (see Introduction, n.1), 2–13.

11. F. Heiler, 'Die Frage der "Absolutheit" des Christentums im Lichte der Religionsgeschichte', *US* 30, 1975, 12.

12. L. Swidler, *After the Absolute. The Dialogical Future of Religious Reflection*, 1990, 7–14. See also L. Swidler and S. Fritsch-Oppermann, 'Was heisst Dialog? Ein Gespräch zwischen einem katholischen Christen und einer evangelischer Christin', in *Engel, Elemente, Energien* (see Introduction, n.3), 121–3. There Swidler writes: 'If up to the last century the understanding of truth in the West was absolute, static, monological or exclusive, since then it has been increasingly de-absolutized and has become dynamic and dialogical, in a word relational.'

13. *Summa Theologica* II–II, Q.1.a.2.

14. P. Knitter, *No Other Name? A Critical Survey of Christian Attitudes Towards the World Religions*, 1984, 219.

15. R. Panikkar, 'Begegnung der Religionen: Das unvermeidliche Gespräch', *Dialog der Religionen* 1, 1991, 16.

16. G. Schneider-Flume, 'Gewissheit und Skepsis. Überlegungen im Anschluss an den exemplarischen Streit zwischen Luther und Erasmus', *Theologische Beiträge* 24, 1993.

17. H. R. Niebuhr, *The Meaning of Revelation*, 1941, 44f.

18. M. von Brück, 'Mystische Erfahrung, religiöse Tradition und die Wahrheitsfrage', in R. Bernhardt, *Horizontüberschreitung* (Ch.9, n.13), 97; also in id., 'Wahrheit und Toleranz im Dialog der Religionen', *Dialog der Religionen* 3, 1993, 14.

19. The 'Guidelines for Dialogue with those of Other Religions and Ideologies' prepared by the WCC in 1979 states: 'Dialogue is . . . a fundamental element of our Christian service to the community. In dialogue, Christians fulfil the commandment: "Love God and your neigbour as yourself"' (quoted from U. Berger and M. Mildenberger [eds.], *Keiner glaubt für sich allein. Theologische Entdeckungen im interreligiösen Dialog*, 1987, 72).

20. W. Pannenberg, 'The Appropriation of the Philosophical Concept of God as a Dogmatic Problem of Early Christian Theology', in *Basic Questions in Theology* 1, 1971, 138.

21. There is an apt English way of expressing the consequences of the recognition of this truth: 'Understanding the truth by standing under the truth.'

22. Schneider-Flume, 'Gewissheit und Skepsis' (n.17), 2.1.

23. R. Ficker, 'Im Zentrum nicht und nicht allein. Von der Notwendigkeit einer Pluralistischen Religionstheologie', in Bernhardt, *Horizontüberschreitung* (Ch.9, n.13), 228. Ficker refers to Gen.32.30; Ex.3.14; Judg.16.6, 17f.; Ex.33.20ff.; I Cor.13.12.

24. See also Mark 10.18.

25. P. Tillich, *Systematic Theology* I, 1951, 136.

26. Cf. Phil.3.12f.: 'Not that I have already obtained this or am already perfect.' Or Rom.8.24: 'For in this *hope* we *were* saved.' See also I Cor.13.12.

27. 'Guidelines' (n.20), 76.

28. Thus a paper produced in 1974 by the mission committee of the Evangelical Church of Germany, published in R. Rendtorff and H. Henrix (eds.), *Die Kirchen und das Judentum. Dokumente von 1945–1985*, 1988, 556.

29. U. Schoen, 'Dialog', in *Lexikon missionstheologischer Grundbegriffe*, 1987, 65f. Cf. also L.Swidler's 'Dialogue Decalogue', in *Ecumenical Review* 33, 1984, 571ff.

30. As an example, mention might be made of the attempt made by the Indian Mogul emperor Akbar the Great (1542–1605), who wanted to see the political unity of India restored through an association of its religions (see H. von Stietencron, 'Geplanter Synkretismus: Kaiser Akbars Religionspolitik', in P. Antes and D. Pahnke [eds.], *Die Religion von Oberschichten. Religion – Profession – Intellektualismus*, 1991, 53–72).

31. Paul J. Griffiths (ed.), *Christianity through Non-Christian Eyes*, 1990, provides valuable help towards the practice of this art.

32. E.g. in 'Toward a Liberation Theology of Religions', in J. Hick (ed.), *The Myth of Christian Uniqueness. Toward a Pluralistic Theology of Religions*, 1987, 178–20; id., 'Religion und Befreiung. Soziozentrismus als Antwort an die Kritiker', in R. Bernhardt, *Horizontüberschreitung* (Ch.9, n.13), 203–19.

33. There have been many suggestions about how Christian–Muslim dialogue should be carried on. See e.g. the section 'Interreligiöse Praxis am Beispiel christlich-islamischer Begegnung in der Bundesrepublik', in *Religionen, Religiosität und christlicher Glaube. Eine Studie der Arnoldshainer Konferenz und der VELKD zum interreligiösen Dialog*, 1991; H.-J. Brandt and C. P. Haase (ed.), *Begegnung mit Türken, Begegnung mit der Islam. Ein Arbeitsbuch*, 1984; EMW (ed.), *Die Begegnung von Christen und Muslimen. Eine Orientierungshilfe*, ²1990; M. Mildenberger, *Kirchengemeinden und ihre muslimischen Nachbarn*, Beitrage zur Ausländerarbeit 13, 1990.

34. S. J. Samartha, 'Mission in einer religiös pluralen Welt', in R. Bernhardt, *Horizontüberschreitung* (Ch.9, n.13), 200.

35. When Karl Rahner was asked by Nishitani, the famous head of the Kyoro school, what he would say if Nishitani described him as an 'anonymous Zen-Buddhist', he replied: 'Certainly you may and must do that from your point of view; I feel myself honoured by such an interpretation' (Rahner, *Theological*

Investigations 16, 1979, 219).

36. I have developed this notion in 'Zur Hermeneutik des interreligiösen Dialogs', *Bibel und Liturgie* 3/92, 131–43.

37. The prohibition against judging one another (Rom.14.10,13) also applies
to dialogue with those of other faiths.

38. R. Friedli offers basic reflections on the search for a criterion for dialogue between the religions in *Fremdheit als Heimat*, 1974.

39. H. Küng, 'Was ist die wahre Religion? Versuche einer ökumenischen Kriteriologie', in H. Deuser et al. (eds.), *Gottes Zukunft – Zukunft der Welt. FS Jürgen Moltmann*, 1986, 536–58: 545.

40. H. Küng, *Global Responsibility* (Preface, n.1), 98.

41. Ibid.

42. H. Gollwitzer, 'Ausser Christus kein Heil?' (Ch.8, n.4), 185f.

43. G. Schmid, *Im Dschungel der neuen Religiosität. Esoterik, östliche Mystik, Sekten, Fundamentalismus, Volkskirchen,* ²1993.

44. I find an evocative expression of this in W. Gern, 'There is no truth which mediates between the religions, but only the truth *in* them which applies to each of them' ('Entwürfe interkultureller Theologie. Ein Buchbericht', *Pastoraltheologie* 79, 1990, 578, 582).

45. C. Westermann, *Isaiah 40–66*, OTL, 1960, 339.

46. I have developed this notion in more detail in 'Deabsolutierung der Christologie?', in M. von Brück and J. Werbick (eds.), *Der einzige Weg zum Heil? Die Herausforderung des christlichen Absolutheitsanspruches durch pluralistische Religionstheologien*, QD 143, 1993, 144–208.

47. G. Bornkamm, *Paul*, 1971, 205.

48. According to P. Tillich, in H. Zahrnt, *Die Sache mit Gott* (Ch. 15, n.38), 385.

49. J. Hick, *God Has Many Names*, 1982, 41.

50. J. Hick, *An Interpretation of Religion. Human Responses to the Transcendent*, 1989, 36ff.

51. J. Ratzinger, 'Das Problem der Absolutheit des christlichen Heilsweges', in W. Böld, *Kirche in der ausserchristlichen Welt*, 1967, 26f.

52. T. Sundermeier, 'Evangelisation und die "Wahrheit der Religionen"', in R. Bernhardt, *Horizontüberschreitung* (Ch. 9, n.13), 184.

53. This terminology is characteristic of the 'fanatics' in the original sense of the word. The original meaning of *fanaticus* is: 'seized by the deity and caught up in raving enthusiasm'.

Index of Names